What People are Saying About

Rescue Me: Tales of Rescuing the Dogs Who Became Our Teachers, Healers, and Always Faithful Friends…

"My name is Jean Owen and I am the owner of NJ Fix My Dog. I have been involved in dog rescue and dog training for over 35 years. I fell in love with *Rescue Me* instantly, It is not only heartwarming, but it is a very needed reminder that there are incredible dogs out there that not only need saving, but can bring such joy, love, and healing to their new family. I had the amazing pleasure of working with Judy and Frances (from a Tale of Two Judys) in building their new relationship and they stole my heart in so many ways!

Dog rescue groups and shelters are an incredible blessing for so many dogs and families. If you are looking to add a new member to your family please be sure you work with a rescue group that performs a thorough temperament test of all of their dogs. Don't adopt a dog unless you are very sure they are the right fit for your family. Sadly, many facilities have gotten so crowded that they are inadvertently placing dogs with aggression issues that no one caught prior to that dog was placed.

Aggression can be worked on, as you will see in the incredible story of Biscuit the Do-Over Dog. I recommend that you know going into the new relationship what the dog's issues are, so they are not a surprise and you can make an informed decision about whether this is the dog for you."

Jean Owen
NJ Fix My Dog

"I absolutely loved the book. There are so many heartwarming warming stories that made me cry tears of joy knowing there are so many others out there who adore and love their fur children as I do. Your wonderful book restores my faith in humanity and tells of the deepest bonds we have with our extended family members, our children...Beautiful, refreshing, book."

Victoria Ansaldo
Rescue Networker

"A poignant book about what happens after a dog leaves a rescue shelter. The dog's life gets better, but so do the lives of the rescuers. From puppies and children, to senior dogs and senior people, *Rescue Me* is inspirational and informative. A great book for any bookshelf."

Charlotte Meade
Meade Canine Rescue Foundation

"The book invites people to look beyond our traditional view of humans rescuing animals and ask the question: "Why is this dog in my life now, what can I learn from him/her?' Because, you know what, rescue is always a two way street and we truly all do better when ALL creatures do better."

Janet Roper
Host of Talk2theAnimals Radio

"An amusing book, seriously written for a very worthy cause. I couldn't put it down. I am very proud of my daughters, Valerie Silver, Geraldine Ambrosio and Judy Ambrosio. If their mother were here, she would be bubbling over with pride."

Ralph "Sonny" Ambrosio
AKC Judge

Rescue Me

Thank you for
helping animals
in need

Val Silver

"2nd" - Dark Photos

Rescue Me

Tales of Rescuing the Dogs Who Became Our Teachers, Healers, and Always Faithful Friends

Val Silver and Team Rescue

Cover by Mary M. Long
http://marymlong.smugmug.com/

Cover Photo of Karal Gregory and Lollipop
Thank You Photo by Karal Gregory and Mary M. Long

All photos in this book are used with permission.

The stories in this book reflect the contributors' recollections of their experiences and their points of view.

ISBN-10: 1493791451
ISBN-13: 978-1493791453

*To you who rescue animals from harm's way,
and help them in ways big and small by
providing refuge, support and forever homes*

Rosie (12), found in the middle of a street, and Bronson (6 1/2), adopted from Friends for Pets. Rescued and loved by Skip and Jennifer Whiting, owners of Wise Tails Pet Boutique, Ojai, CA.

Saving one dog may not save the world, but it will surely change the world for that one dog.

~Author Unknown

Table of Contents

Accompanying companion guide, audios, videos, and more
available at tapinfinity.com/rescue-me/

ACKNOWLEDGMENTS

Special thanks to the Team Rescue contributors for sharing their heartwarming stories and their ongoing encouragement and support. You are my inspiration and my heroes; you have taught me so much. Thank you also to Geraldine Ambrosio for assisting with editing, Mary M. Long for creating the cover and working with me ever so patiently until we got it right, and to Jennifer Whiting for her copyrighting assistance.

INTRODUCTION

After losing my precious French Bulldog, Louis, I found myself crying daily while perusing petfinder.com looking at homeless dog photos. So many faces filled the pages, and the needs of the organizations caring for them appeared overwhelming. I knew the gifts I made to the local shelter were valuable, but they seemed so small in the face of such great need. I kept thinking of the story of the boy saving dying starfish by throwing them back into the ocean, one at a time, as he walked along the beach. Even though there were so many, and he could only save a few, he did not give up. He knew his efforts mattered to the ones he saved.

So I prayed, "What can I do?"

The idea for this book came to me in a flash of inspiration; write about how we rescue dogs and how they rescue us and make our lives better in return; get other dog lovers to tell their stories, too; donate the profits to several organizations so they can worry less about money and focus on healing, saving, re-homing, and creating better conditions for the animals in their care. It sounded daunting, and yet I knew I could do it and had to do my part.

Let's be honest. People have created a big problem for companion animals, and it will take a concerted commitment by people to make it better. Until then, countless millions will continue to suffer. Pet overpopulation caused by over-breeding and refusing to spay and neuter has created a situation where there are simply not enough good homes for all the animals in need of them. Often, those who had families find themselves homeless by no fault of their own. Some are removed from neglectful, abusive owners. Others are abandoned after losing their puppy cuteness, or when they get too big or too old. Perhaps the novelty wears off or they get too expensive. Some get dumped when the family moves or a human baby comes along. Hunting dogs may be released at season's end. Puppy mill mommas are thrown away when they are no longer cash machines. Sometimes, caring owners are forced by circumstances beyond their control to tearfully surrender their beloved companions.

For all these reasons, homeless dogs need refuge. For some, a shelter is a welcomed change from foraging on the streets or being chained up, abused or neglected. More often they enter feeling scared, alone, confused and sad. Why did their family leave them? They wait hopefully in small kennels for their people to come back. They wait for someone to take them home and love them. Some wait months or years. They may not know that they are the lucky ones. In some areas, dogs enter a shelter only to find themselves facing a horrific gas chamber death or a heart stopping injection within a matter of days or weeks—hardly enough time to even be adopted. Rescue workers work tirelessly to relocate and find homes for these dogs, but there are so many, too many. Of the six to eight million dogs and cats cared for by shelters every year, three to four million are euthanized because there is no room for them all. A quarter of them are purebreds. Countless more die abandoned or at the hands of their owners.

It is for those dogs and their rescuers that we wrote this book. Our goals are threefold: to raise funds for then, just finding them forever homes dedicated to caring for homeless animals and finding them forever homes, to raise awareness of the needs and worthiness of homeless animals, and to encourage pet owners to be responsible, committed, loving caregivers to the pets who have so much to offer them when given the chance.

The twelve stories in this book are written by ordinary people with extraordinary hearts and touching tales of how rescued dogs became precious members of their families, and how they have become better, happier people for it. We hope your heart is touched by the spirits of these dogs just as ours are.

Val Silver

THE PUPPY IN A NEWSPAPER SACK

"Mom! Come here!"

I knew by the tone of their voices calling from the driveway that my two sons, Jim and Sean, were in possession of an animal they didn't dare bring into the house. My only guess was what kind. And I confess my first impulse was to not even look, to just turn away.

We had already been through a long string of gerbils, hamsters and guinea pigs. Our recently adopted cat was the latest addition to the family. He finished off the last hamster and became my responsibility after the novelty of caring for him wore off.

I left the dirty dinner dishes and peered down the stairs through the open door to the driveway. "What is it?" I called back.

There they stood with their big tan newspaper sacks slung across their bodies. Paper route complete, the bags should have been empty. Sean reached into his sack and pulled out a little gray and black spotted puppy. One look at him confirmed the obvious. He wasn't somebody's puppy gone astray. He appeared to be around two months old and couldn't have weighed five pounds. With hip bones already protruding, it was also certain that he wouldn't survive much longer on his own.

"Bring him in, and give him a flea bath right away," I commanded. I should have known better than to expect two inexperienced preteens to do a good job of it, but my attention was on kitchen cleanup after a long day at work, not on that poor little stray.

Sean was immediately taken with the wiry-haired puppy. "We aren't keeping him," I said. One look at his feet and coat told me he was going to grow up big and hairy. As a single working mother my plate was already full. "Tomorrow, I'm calling the SPCA."

Despite how skinny he was, the puppy wouldn't eat, and that had me worried. I knew in my gut something was wrong. Thoughts of possible dog diseases went through my head and I worried this rescue would not end well.

After the boys went to bed, Spots and I sat together on the floor. Thankfully, he nibbled a little boiled chicken from my hand while sitting in my lap. As we sat there, I reran the boys' story in my head. They were walking down the street, finishing up their paper route when he started following them. They knew he needed help, so my youngest son, twelve year old Sean, scooped him up and put him in his sack. Even though I wasn't thrilled to have a puppy around, I was very proud of my boys and touched by the compassion they showed.

I could only imagine what he went through. *Was he dumped? How did he feel being on the streets alone? Where was his mother and where would he find something to eat?*

The late September nights were getting cold, and a

little pup like him didn't stand much of a chance on his own. But then, just when the situation was about to become hopeless, two lanky boys appeared and changed his destiny. They must have felt safe and friendly because he followed them. Maybe he had followed others, we don't know. This time though, it was different. These boys didn't turn away. They took him home.

As I rubbed under his chin, my intuition gnawed at me. Something just did not feel right. His skin felt *crusty*. I grabbed the cat's flea comb and ran it through his chest hairs. To my horror half the comb was filled with big brown clumps of flea dirt, blood and fleas.

"Get the flea soap." I yelled up the stairs, and into my nice clean sink he went. Hundreds of fleas washed away. I have never seen anything like it. No wonder he was so lethargic. He was already weak and hungry from lack of food. The fleas were taking what little life he had left.

Once he was free of fleas, we could only hope for the best. I went to bed, not knowing what morning would bring. I wanted to get down to him before the boys got up, just in case our intervention was too late. To my great relief, a wagging tail and a voracious appetite greeted me as I rounded the last few steps to the kitchen. Little Spots was a new dog.

After two weeks of loving him and trying to get him into the shelter, we all got attached to him. When there was finally an opening, the little boy pleas and tears easily won me over. I caved in on two conditions. Sean would be his primary caretaker, and he needed a new name.

Duke, the newspaper sack puppy, had found his forever home.

. . .

This story, however, isn't only about our compassion

towards Duke. His compassion for others outweighed anything we ever did for him. He touched many with his kind, gentle, yet funny ways. As he grew older, people were especially drawn in by his eyes, and they would inevitably exclaim about what a wise old soul he appeared to be.

Until getting to know Duke, I had thought of compassion as primarily a human or divine trait. Sure I had heard stories of animal heroism, but this was different. Duke was kind in small ways. His kindness extended to us even during times we had been unworthy of it. One such recipient of his good nature was our incredibly selfish, full of himself French Bulldog, Louis.

Lou joined our family when Duke was around four years old. I'll never forget the first time they met. Duke was outside when we pulled into the driveway with Lou. As soon as he saw us emerge together from the car, his happy demeanor changed. He began snorting and stomping around the yard as if to say, *"Are you KIDDING me?"* Being an exceptionally intelligent dog, he must have known what was coming. If I could read his mind, my guess would be that he was upset about another dog taking our attention.

. . .

Over time, our fur boys became best buddies; they enjoyed many hours of tug-o-war and long walks together. Lou loved Duke, but when it came to kindness, the street ran in only one direction. Still, Duke cared for the little boss, even when that care had been abused.

There were two occasions in particular when Duke completely awed us with his compassion towards Louis. While visiting family for the holidays, he played happily with the only available toy as Lou sat watching, quite bored and unhappy. After a few minutes, Duke walked over to Lou, and let one end of the dumbbell drop from his mouth. That they would share the toy had to be wishful thinking on his part. In typical fashion, Lou grabbed on, yanked the toy from Duke's mouth, and ran off. Duke accepted this and found something else to do. We all watched in amazement, singing his praises. Years later, we still talk about that night.

He topped this act a few summers later when we were enjoying play time on the shore of Lake Ontario. Duke was a natural water dog who glided through the water with the grace of a ballerina. Lou could barely hold his head above water and would frantically swim, eyes bulging, until his feet touched bottom. He preferred wading on the rock slabs and fetching sticks in shallow waters. One time, I threw Lou's stick a little too far and the waves carried it out of reach. To Duke's delight, he safely possessed both sticks. This scene didn't last long. In characteristic fashion, Duke could not ignore Lou's longing look and he did the most incredible thing. He gave one of the sticks a push towards shore with his mouth. Lou eagerly waded out and grabbed it. And yes, when Duke came back to shore with his stick, Lou took that one too.

. . .

Duke was a friend to all of us no matter what. His antics, foibles, dorky quirks (like sleeping in Lou's little bed when he had his own big bed), and happy spirit made me laugh at times when little else could. How could I not laugh when he would throw his big, wet, smelly self onto my lap after having a good roll on a dead carp? Of course, his very favorite time to do that was after a bath–no sweet smelling fur for Duke!

One of Dukey's foibles was stealing items. He so loved tissues that one of his nicknames was "McTissue". Even as he grew weak and winded with metastasized thyroid cancer, he made me laugh one last time when I spotted him in the yard with a small pair of mounted antlers. His antler 'smile' looked so funny I just had to catch him on video.

At almost 15 years old, on Friday the 13th of March, 2010, it was once again Duke's turn to be on the receiving end of our compassion. This time, there was no easy fix. I prayed every day that he would pass away peacefully in his sleep so I wouldn't have to make that awful, fateful decision. Taking him to the vet for that shot was one of the hardest things I've ever had to do. Later that night, when I awakened from a fitful sleep, there was a very different feeling in my room. It was as if I was in an energetically palpable void that literally took my breath away. My eyes popped open and I said, "Oh. My God." Lou was snuggled beside me, but the room felt so dark and *so empty*. It was only then that I really truly realized the magnitude of Duke's soul and how his life force filled our home without us even knowing it.

As I look back over my life with Duke, I have to wonder. Was it coincidence or an act of the divine that made him follow my sons? A puppy, let alone one that would grow into a big, hairy dog, was not in my plans. Yet there he was. I used to think we rescued Duke, but it is perhaps more true that in so many ways he rescued us. He was always there when we needed a friend, showed us how to live and love life in the moment, and was an example of extending grace to the undeserving. We are so grateful to have shared our lives with this wonderful soul. He will always have a place in our hearts and we are better people for having known him.

Story by Val Silver

It came to me that every time I lose a dog they take a piece of my heart with them. And every new dog who comes into my life gifts me with a piece of their heart. If I live long enough, all the components of my heart will be dog, and I will become as generous and loving as they are.

~Author Unknown

A TALE OF TWO JUDYS

In April 2007, I had very mixed emotions about adopting a dog. My travel and work schedule was hectic, and I was afraid of making another long commitment. While owning a dog is fulfilling, I knew too well the pain of losing one.

While traveling down to Maryland with my friend Joyce, and talking about it in the car I said, "Well, what does it hurt just to look and see what's out there." Of course, those were just cover up words for, "I really want a dog to love, but don't want to admit it to myself or anyone else." If I were to take the leap and find a new best friend, certain conditions needed to be met. The dog had to be small, a girl, and friendly.

My mission started at the Humane Society of Kent County in Chestertown, Maryland. We were greeted by a very friendly staff, who directed us to the bulletin board featuring photos of all the available dogs. Many were hounds, but a photo of a Short Haired Collie grabbed my attention. She seemed to light up the board.

When I went to the kennel to meet her, she was jumping up and down on her door as though to say, "Pick me! Pick me!" One look at this bundle of energy made it clear she was not for me. I told her, "I'm sorry, you are just too big. I wish you luck and hope you find a nice home."

As we were getting ready to leave for another shelter, something peculiar happened. The director said, "You know the name on her photo says Lady, but her real name is Judy." Why she said that I do not know. There was no way she could have known that my name is Judy. My friend, no stranger to the sometimes strange turn of events my life takes, thought this so weird that she needed to sit down for a minute. "Do you realize this dog not only has your name, but also your energy?" she asked.

Regardless of her name, I decided to travel twenty more miles to another shelter in search of the small, friendly female I thought I wanted. When we arrived there, I began to realize the wheels of fate had already been set in motion. I hurried through the building, barely looking at the dogs; all I cared about was getting back to Chestertown before my namesake could be adopted by someone else.

It was a beautiful Saturday morning and the Humane Society was busy. In desperation, I had Joyce drive while I filled out the application. When we arrived, I literally ran into the building to see if Judy was still there. The director said, "I knew you'd be back. The two of you are made for each other." WOW! I breathed a big sigh of relief. A volunteer threw up his arms and said, "Yeah, she got a home!"

Now the technical stuff started. I needed to satisfy the requirements for the adoption. Judy was very attentive, not missing a move, as she and Joyce sat waiting in a holding room. The director worked on the police and veterinary files. Everything was approved, but there was one small problem standing in the way. The tax office was closed and unless we could verify that I owned a home, she had to stay at the shelter. Judy was not an apartment dog.

Even though the director said she would hold her for me until everything was approved and I could return to pick her up, it was more difficult than it sounded. I lived four hours away and I work long hours. I was heartbroken and Judy knew it. Her ears went back and she stopped wagging her tail.

When I told my friend what happened she jumped up and vouched for me, but that was not enough to meet the requirements. At that moment, an idea popped into my head, "What about my accountant?" I was so excited when Marion answered the phone. "Wait a minute," I said. "Someone needs to talk to you."

Her reply was typical of our long friendship. She said, "Judy, what are you up to, now?"

The other Judy, not missing a beat, saw the situation improving, and quickly perked up. By now I was reassuring her and telling her about her new home in New Jersey. We quickly finished the paperwork, bought a leash and collar, and headed off.

Now the issue became her name. Family and friends agreed; no house was big enough for two energetic Judys. That problem was also about to be solved in a most unusual way. After showing my new best buddy around Chestertown before our drive back to New Jersey, the question of her name was foremost on my mind. Lo and behold, who did we meet on that memorable Saturday evening but two priests also out for a walk. They petted the dog, and like most dog lovers asked her name. As I explained the situation, one of the priests smiled and said she was a blessing from Saint Francis. Later, as we were driving home on the turnpike, Joyce suggested that I name her Frances, after Saint Francis, the patron saint of animals. That was it! She liked her new name and so did I.

. . .

Because this was her third home in her short year of life, it was not surprising that Frances had issues to overcome. Her first visit to the vet revealed a lung worm infection that left scar tissue. She would not go up and down stairs, and would only walk on flat surfaces. It was six months before she would even touch the bathroom tile; trucks and loud noises scared her.

Eventually, she overcame her fears and her health improved. However, some dislikes remain constant. Motorcycles, police cars, and pizza delivery cars send her into fits of barking and dire feelings of aggravation. Pedicures are also problematic. When I walk her to the Maywood Veterinary Clinic, she knows it's nail clipping time. As soon as we reach the vet's street, the drama begins. Her whole body freezes and she will not budge. The only way I can get her inside is to carry her, stiff-bodied with legs sticking straight out. The first time the veterinary assistant saw this she started yelling, "Doctor Buchholz, hurry there's an emergency!" Yes, there was an emergency, especially since carrying a 45 pound dog in that position is no easy feat.

. . .

Frances is clearly different from any other dog I've owned. Spending time with her and talking to her is motivating. My corporate job and home life are often very stressful. When I get home and open the door, there she is. She waits, not to be loved, but to give me love. It seems as if she says, "How was your day? Whenever you are ready, I am ready for our four mile power walk." During my most tiresome times, she is there for me, not letting me go it alone. She has taught me that I was really the one who needed to be rescued. She taught me not to be selfish with my time, and that I don't have to run home to get on a treadmill or run to the gym by myself because our time together is much more meaningful.

Frances has taught me to be more balanced in life. She taught me how to get out and share my time with others. Because of her, I've met some very nice people in agility training and other classes we've taken together. We enjoy power walking along with her best dog friend, Jasmine. She became certified as a therapy dog so we could visit the residents in nursing homes.

After our first visit to the facility, I cried the entire way home. I told her we would not be doing that again. But what I realized as I looked at her in the rear view mirror was that she was happy. There she was in the back seat wagging her tail as though to say, "Hey, we helped people today and made them smile." That was another lesson. It dawned on me that for some of the sick she is their only visitor. How could I take that away from them?

When my mother passed away, Frances was there for me. She sensed my sadness and showed me love as only she could. While dozing on and off in bed one night, I felt her jumping on and off my bed. This was odd behavior because usually she just lays there. Thinking she was being disturbed by my restlessness, I told her I was sorry for being such lousy company. Finally, she lay down next to me with her chin on my stomach. When I opened my eyes, I discovered what she had been up to. I found myself surrounded by stuffed toys. "What's this?" I asked her. The poor thing carried six of her most favorite toys, including her beloved Mr. Snowman, from downstairs up to my room. That is why she kept jumping on and off the bed.

Words could not describe how I felt. I cried in happiness as I hugged and snuggled her. Here I was, once again, on the receiving end of her unconditional, healing love. She gave from her heart and comforted me within the circle of her most loved possessions. As I thanked her for her gifts of love, it was apparent that my best friend, my shadow, my queen, clearly rescued me. We are a team through good times and bad, when we are happy or sad, active or taking it easy. Day and night we have each other.

Story by Judy Ambrosio

I RESCUED A HUMAN TODAY

Her eyes met mine as she walked down the corridors peering apprehensively into the kennels. I felt her need instantly, and knew I had to help her. I wagged my tail, not too exuberantly, so she wouldn't be afraid.

As she stopped at my kennel, I blocked her view from a little accident I had in the back of my cage. I didn't want her to know that I hadn't been walked today. Sometimes, the overworked shelter keepers get too busy, and I didn't want her to think poorly of them.

As she read my kennel card, I hoped that she wouldn't feel sad about my past. I only have the future to look forward to, and want to make a difference in someone's life.

She got down on her knees, and made little kissy sounds at me. I shoved my shoulder and side of my head against the bars to comfort her. Gentle fingertips caressed my neck; she was desperate for companionship. A tear fell down her cheek, and I raised my paw to assure her that all would be well.

Soon my kennel door opened and her smile was so bright that I jumped into her arms.

I would promise to keep her safe.

I would promise to always be by her side.

I would promise to do everything I could to see that radiant smile and sparkle in her eyes.

I was so fortunate that she came down my corridor. So many more to be saved. At least I could save one.

I rescued a human today.

Written by Janine Allen CPDT, Rescue Me Dog's professional dog trainer. Janine's passion is working with people and their dogs. She provides demonstrations for those who have adopted shelter dogs, lends email support to adopted dog owners that need information beyond our Training Support Pages, and aids shelter staff and volunteers in understanding dog behavior to increase their adoptability. See this article at http://rescuemedog.org/dog-blog/i-rescued-a-human-today-by-janine-allen/ Copyright 2013 Rescue Me Dog; www/rescuemedog.org

Photo of Judy Ambrosio and Frances

A PASSION FOR RESCUE

My name is Julia Buie, and for the last four years, I have been a shelter and rescue dog activist and volunteer. I have always been an animal lover, but it was only when my family started asking, "Who are you?" and I started asking myself that same question, that my mother reminded me of this forgotten side of myself; how I was the child who brought in the 'scroungies' from the time I could walk. She told me about two of my rescues starting from the ripe old age of toddlerhood. First, there was the tiny sparrow with a broken leg. She healed and was allowed to hop from plate to plate on the dinner table, picking off whatever she wanted. A cat with mange came next; the same cat that eventually ended up killing the sparrow.

It would take fifty years and a twist in fate to rekindle my passion for animals in need in a rather miraculous way. I had recently discovered Facebook, and started reconnecting with some of my old friends. About two weeks later, as I was scrolling down my page, I saw a post from the Pet Pardons page showing a photo of a German shepherd type dog on death row needing to be saved. Because of my passion for animals, I clicked on the link to find out what it was all about. I saw that thousands of people belonged to this group; their mission is to save the lives of homeless dogs from around the country.

What was particularly odd is that I did not know how this post got on my feed. None of my friends sent it. I did not know the woman posting it, nor did she know me. I told myself this had to be an act of God. It was my wake-up call because I never knew what horrors were taking place in animal shelters. That is when my journey into the 'real' world began.

The next thing I knew I was sharing their dog posts on my own page. My passion got a hold of me and I started writing words filled with tears, anger, and empathy. I lost many old friends who didn't want to read about this, but my words eventually connected me with over 1300 animal loving friends who also shared my passion to save dogs and cats before their time was up. Some fought tirelessly all day, every day, for changes to be made for shelter and abused animals.

Every night I looked at the photos of who got saved, who got euthanized, and some of those faces you would just fall in love with. I cried and cried.

My husband said, "Honey, you're spending an awful lot of time on the computer with those animals. You have to stop crying like this. That's no good for you."

And I would bring him into the room and say, "Look at these faces. How sad is that?" There were the cruelty cases, and the emaciated animals, and just the beautiful faces in the shelter and people pleading for their lives.

. . .

It was my husband who suggested that I go to our local shelter to help them out. Within two months of volunteering, my passion got hold of me like a whirlwind and I became a one woman fundraiser. For two weeks, I baked brownies, cookies, cakes, muffins and loaf cakes to freeze. The day before my event, I thawed and frosted until each and every item was done. I scoured yard sales for pretty cake plates and platters to adorn the baked items on and even found time to enlist small local groups to help sell them for me. I went to businesses within the county looking for gift certificates and other items for donation that I could raffle off. Being that I was in the antiques and collectibles business, I also donated a lot of items for the silent auction.

In the one day I did this, I raised $700. I used this money to buy much needed vaccines, medications and other necessities because my shelter had hardly any funding for these items. The people from the shelter were flabbergasted because they had never seen anything like this. They were like, "Who are you?"

My family was just amazed, too. "Who are you?" they asked.

I thought, "Well, I don't know." Apparently, I was just finding out myself. I was not like this. I was not that outgoing and every day I just say thank you to God because he must have done this. He knew I needed something in my life.

All I know is that I got real sad, real angry, real frustrated, and then I got real busy.

. . .

It was while I was hosting my fundraiser that I met my best friend, Patricia. As the shelter's volunteer rescue coordinator, she worked around the clock finding rescues to take our shelter dogs and cats before their time was up. This was when I knew rescue is what I also wanted to do and we became a force to be reckoned with. Together, we kept the shelter's rescue rate at 100%. No adoptable dogs were killed.

Successful rescue requires a network of people; foster care, grooming, re-homing, transportation, donations for veterinary care, and finding help for special cases are all part of it. In my rural area, people willing to help out are hard to come by. When you are really involved in this movement, you can't stand back and say, "Oh, well." Patricia and I do whatever needs doing.

That's how Buddy became a member of our family. My mother called to tell me about her elderly neighbor and friend, Irene, who had been found dead in her home. And could I take her dog Buddy because he had no one else. He was a six year old fat little whale with a mouthful of crooked teeth. Irene and Buddy had a passion for cheesecake and eventually he became diabetic and blind. But, oh, I had always wanted a pug, so we added him to our pack of two dogs to make a beautiful three pack. My husband was smitten with Buddy, too.

From the first night, Buddy took to sleeping between my legs on the bed. He scratched on me as if to say, "Spread 'em!" He was never allowed on Irene's bed; he had his own bed on the floor. Come to find out Irene stretched out on the recliner every night and his spot was between her legs. Buddy just left us due to cancer at the ripe age of 16. He was our precious baby boy, the love of our lives. It is hard for me to sleep without him.

Gracie, a boxer and pit bull mix came along next. By this time we had already lost Jolie to cancer. She arrived on the 2:00 AM train from Georgia for me to foster until she found her very own home. Sadly, I became a foster failure. We fell in love with Gracie and there was no way we could send her away. After all, no one would have loved her better.

My husband no longer allows me to foster, but that didn't stop me from taking care of dogs in need. A couple of years ago, four feral puppies came into the shelter. The best we could figure, they were from two Chow mix mothers who were part of a dog pack that was running around Smithfield for the last 10 years. The pups were supposed to be euthanized because it was suspected that they had sarcoptic mange, which is very contagious to dogs and humans, and at that time the shelter had no quarantine room. They looked so scared and pathetic with their loss of hair. I just had to save their lives.

The director said, "Julia, no."

I said, "Uh, uh, uh, don't tell me no, not on my watch."

He gave me 24 hours to find a place for those puppies. I contacted my neighbor, who agreed to let them stay in his unused back yard kennels for two weeks. Two weeks turned into two months. Every day, three to four times a day in the dead heat of summer, I went over in a rubber suit to treat their mange. I worked hard to familiarize them with human touch. I gave them their vaccines and got them spayed or neutered. When they were about five to six months old, they were just about tame enough to be adopted out, and adopted out they were. We kept Fonzy, the biggest one and the least tamed. He does everything a 'normal' dog does; he just doesn't like it when you reach out to pet him. It frightens him, so he pulls back and might run out the doggy door. Sometimes I trap him inside, and then I'm able to rub him all over an even give him kisses.

The last dog to join our pack was Moo-Moo, the basset hound. He got his name from birth. He opened his mouth and made this God-awful sound. If you could hear him, you would know what I mean. We rescued him in a different way. He was living in a crate 14-16 hours a day and the owner could no longer keep him. My sister-in-law (who had his mother) called and asked us to take him. Believe it or not my husband said, "Why not!"

Everybody loves the Moo-Moo, even though he's obnoxious and tattles on the other dogs. He runs into my room, sits, and bellows on and on. I'd say, "Stop, that's obnoxious, stop!" It took about five times of this before I finally decided to follow him when he races out of the room. Sure enough, Fonzy and Gracie were getting into trouble. They have been caught tearing my clothes off the clothesline and eating shoes and furniture. It took two years for them to grow out of their destructive phase. I love those thrift stores. Now I know when Moo-Moo comes in and bellows like a banshee I get right up and follow him. He tells the truth every time!

. . .

My husband doesn't share my passion for rescue, but he understands and supports me. I am not allowed any more dogs of my own. He now turns red in the face if I'm within five miles down the road and mention the word dog. He tells me, "If you come within a mile of this house with a dog, it's over." I used to think he was kidding but then I caught on that he means it! I think he actually regrets ever suggesting that I go help our local shelter.

I had to explain to him how this made me a whole person. Fourteen years ago, I was diagnosed as bipolar, and probably have been all of my life. Now that I take medication my whole life has changed. Being the 'Voice for the Voiceless' is actually what has made me complete. This has been the best medicine ever. Yes, there has been a lot of stress, there's been a lot of heartbreak, a ton of tears, but then there's that reward at the end of the day when you know you have done everything possible to help save an animal, sometimes several. I wouldn't change my life for the world.

When I pick up a shelter dog for transport, I get a very

special feeling; I can't even explain it. My heart swells with joy, and I feel giddy all over. I talk soothingly to the dog, and give it love, maybe for the first time ever. I say, "You have got a second chance and you are on your way to a good life." This is so amazing to be part of that.

People just don't know until they get into this, how heartbreaking rescue work can be. I've heard some have even taken their own lives over the pain and suffering animals go through. You can't let it break you like that; you have to be stronger because this is difficult. It can consume your life. Who knew? I plan on doing what I do until the day they find me slumped over my computer with all the life gone from my body. I know that when I die God will be glad to have me on his side. And I know that my beloved babies who have crossed over wait for me at the Rainbow Bridge.

In my lifetime I pray that we will have become a 'No-kill Nation', and that everyone becomes educated on spaying and neutering. This is the only way it will ever end.

Story by Julia Buie as told to Val Silver
Audio available on webpage

He is your friend, your partner, your defender, your dog. You are his life, his love, his leader. He will be yours, faithful and true, to the last beat of his heart. You owe it to him to be worthy of such devotion.

~Author Unknown

Photo of Julia Buie with Gracie and Moo-Moo

I care not for a man's religion whose dog and cat are not the better for it.

~Abraham Lincoln

LOLLIPOP CAN'T HOLD HER LICKER

Oh. My. Gawd. Your dog looks just like Gene Simmons.

A thick skin comes in handy when you work in animal rescue, but it doesn't always come naturally. Often, it's cultivated layer by layer, dog by dog, an invisible but necessary armor against constant exposure to the elements of neglect, abandonment, and abuse. A tough hide protects your heart enough to allow you to continue, yet it cannot become so hardened that it prevents the soul of the animals from shining through. We rescue, rehab, re-home and reintroduce dogs to the lives they so deserve, but we are also here to be their voice and a means of education, awareness, and change.

So when I'm out with my girls and hear caustic comments about my slack-jawed beagle with the droopy tongue, I hold *mine* long enough to put reactive defenses aside and explain that Lollipop, mouth wide open like a funhouse-entrance clown, can't hold *hers*.

Most people, like the woman who burst out laughing

as she compared her to Gene Simmons of KISS, find humor in her floppy-faced appearance. But there are other times, when we're walking down the beach and her sand-covered tongue is swinging and slapping her cheeks with each step, that murmured judgments and not so quiet accusations about how I *really need to give that dog some water* travel over the sand and sting both my ears and my heart.

By far, my favorite interactions are with children. They see Lolli's licker and their eyes grow wide. Usually the first thing they say is something along the lines of, *"Hey Lady! What's wrong with your dog?!"* They ask their questions with honest fascination: *How do you feed her? Can she drink water? Does it hurt?*

Lolli laps up the attention while I explain that her bottom jawbone was broken and a nasty infection took most of her teeth. I tell them about the wonderful animal doctor who rescued her after she was dropped off at the shelter, and fixed her up as best he could. We discuss how, without bottom teeth, her tongue won't stay in her mouth–so it lolls out, all the time, like licking an invisible lollipop. Drinking water is easy but she can't chew, so I mush soft food into little footballs that she sucks down like an ATM eating a debit card. I tell them that it used to hurt a little but it doesn't anymore. That now she's very, very happy. This is only partially true, but some things kids just don't need to know.

They don't need to know that her jawbone was brutally ripped from her head, torn clean away and left hanging from her face. That so much time passed between when she was injured and when she got help that she was down to skin and bones. That she suffered unimaginable pain because her former owner "thought it

28

would heal on its own."

I've often wondered why, in an area where outdoor dogs are the norm and hunting strays abound, she wasn't just shot and put out of her misery. I suspect it had something to do with her eyes—the same eyes that melted the staff at the Lynchburg Humane Society in charge of deciding her fate. "I was ready to put her down," he said, "but something in her eyes told me she wanted to live."

Those eyes got me too, pleading up at me from my friend's email. Brenda was well aware of my reputation for rescuing misfit hounds, beginning in 2002 with Pearl, a rickety old Beagle who wandered into my parent's yard and refused to leave. Her message was, "She's your kind of dog!"

With the stability and security of a wayward gypsy, one old hound already sharing my tiny garage apartment, and a tendency to be self-centered and lazy, the only other dog allowed in my space was the small figurine of a hound I'd found on the beach one summer day with Pearl. Still, I couldn't ignore that face staring back at me. Big, milky-brown eyes gazed sadly and shyly from between long, silky ears; soft white muzzle, dotted with specks of brown, surrounded her hound-sized sniffer; the fur between her brows grew down the center of her snout like a tiny Mohawk. And then there was that tongue, hanging lazily from her broken, crooked little mouth, blowing the photographer a raspberry.

I drove four hours to Lynchburg and spent 10 minutes with a dog so broken in spirit that she stood with her head down in defeat and refused to look at me.

Yep, my kind of dog.

. . .

Her eyes may have kept her alive, but her ordeal left her

extremely traumatized. Away from the safety of Dr. Henry's cozy kennel, she was scared of everyone and everything. Too unsure and intimidated to explore her surroundings, she spent most of her first day home peeing in the house-five times on the floors and once in the center of my bed.

Then there were the surgeries. Starting several months before she came to me, and continuing over the next two years, Lolli's vet performed several major operations in an effort to save and repair her face. Most involved removing dead bone fragments and cleaning out recurring infection. Then we implanted metal plates in her jaw to stabilize her mouth for eating and give her a more normal appearance. When the screws holding the plates failed, we tried using pins. When one of the pins broke loose and sprung up through her gums (think punk rock pooch), we once again went back to plates.

Poor Lolli took the slips and pops and the swollen face and stitches in stride. As she healed, she also began to trust, doing more of the things beagles are supposed to do. She wagged her tail, slept on my bed, went for walks, and sat in the car with her head–and her tongue–out the window. She could eat and drink by herself, and she didn't seem to mind that her sassy little licker switched sides after each operation.

Still, she seemed stiff and sad, and her face looked pained and worried. Sometimes, she acted downright depressed, lying around and staring up at me with sad puppy eyes. I started to question my motives when a physical therapist friend mentioned that the hardware in her head might be causing some muscular misalignment and migraines. Why were we doing this to help her if it caused her discomfort? Was it about function, or was there an underlying, ulterior agenda of form? Was I trying too hard to create a face that conformed to the norm and sacrificing her soul in the process?

The answer became clear on a trip to the beach, where she and Pearl often ran through the dunes. Waves from a recent storm had sliced the slope from the dune line and left an abrupt vertical drop in its place. As usual, Lolli came crashing through the sea grass, head held high, ears and tongue flapping freely. This time, though, she was caught off guard. I watched as she went flying off the cliff and somersaulted mid-air, landing squarely on top of her head. The thought of her jerry-rigged jaw bending backwards caused my stomach to do a few flip-flops of its own. My heart stopped, but Lolli simply sat down and stared at me. A little dazed, she shook her head from side to side, rattling her chin and slapping her tongue against her cheeks as if to say *Wake up! Get over it! Get back in the ring, Rocky!* And then she was off, once more running like the wind. As quickly as it happened, it was done.

Shortly after, the metal plates failed again. I talked to Lolli's vet and we agreed there would be no more surgeries. It was time to let Lolli live her life *au naturel*. We finished our work with one final procedure, removing the plates and placing a few stitches on both sides of her mouth to pull up the floppy chin.

. . .

Free from the hardware, her personality blossomed. Both her face and her demeanor relaxed, and she became the dog she was meant to be. Instead of hesitant hellos, she now greets me with her bouncy beagle dance. She plays, sniffs stinky stuff, and rolls in stinkier stuff. Bowls of popcorn are not safe in her presence, and though she can't actually chew her food, she's learned to use her nose to roll things onto her paw, up her arm, and into her mouth. Every morning she starts the day with her tail-wagging butt poised playfully in the air. Every night she lies beside me while I read and watch TV. And everywhere, at every moment, there is that tongue.

I thought I was fixing Lolli's face with the hardware, but what I know now is that she never really needed it. My intentions were good, but maybe I did it more for myself than for her. Lolli is simply Lolli, and she doesn't care if being who she is causes someone else to laugh. She doesn't care what anyone thinks about her tongue any more than she cares that she slobbers in her sleep and wakes me with the shrill trumpet sound of her snores. She's not perfect, but neither does she hide behind artificiality in an attempt to conform to what is expected or what is the norm.

She is so resilient. Even though she bears the wounds and scars from her previous life, she hasn't let them harden her heart. I've learned that unlike dogs who adapt to their circumstances, I often feel compelled to control, to almost *force* my fate through stability and structure. I have seen how we humans choose to live propped against a false sense of security, rather than trusting that we might thrive if we tear down the plates and pins, allowing our dreams to flap loosely in the wind. I have come to understand that if we let go and fly off the cliff, we'd have to rely on something more esoteric yet stronger than any delusional structure we could ever create: we would have to rely on *faith*.

Lolli feeds my faith and shares my kindred gypsy soul. She's traveled with me from Virginia to California twice and shown me that if I leap and land on my head, I'll bounce back. She's taught me that *different* doesn't mean *broken* and that it's better not to conform when your soul is yearning to break free. Her joy at simple things like breakfast and the beach make me laugh 'til I cry. Her unflappable spirit, warm body, and soft fur have comforted me, the way only a dog truly can, through those changes and losses that bruise the heart.

I wake each day to her body curled between my thighs, and when I lie down at night she flops beside me. Draping her neck over mine, she whines and wiggles to get closer, smothering my face with her own. There, in the warm folds of her skin, her soft, wet tongue against my cheek, I feel her heart.

Story by Karal Gregory

EPILOGUE

In June of 2013, Lolli got sick. She began having seizures and we let her go to the Rainbow Bridge. It is likely that she had a brain lesion or tumor, as the seizures were increasing in length and severity. She was an old girl, estimated near 13, but still very full of life and love. As dogs do, she seemed to have a sense of what was coming as she spent her last night curled up beside me, resting her face on my shoulder.

I hand fed her twice a day for seven years, chewed up more treats for her than I can count, nursed her through more than ten jaw surgeries, and flipped her chin so it would face back in the right direction while she slept. I saw her blossom from an abused and scared little hound to a bouncy beagle full of life. I will miss her. No one's best friend is ever 'just a dog'.

Until one has loved an animal, a part of one's soul remains unawakened.

~Anatole France

JUJU~OUR HEART SONG

The day Juju came into our lives started with a veterinary wellness visit for our pug, Miss Puckles. She has been the love of our lives and queen of her domain since her birth in 2006. Puckles was having a grand time watching all the critters come and go from the waiting room. She seemed especially interested in the big boys, although most didn't give her as much as a sniff.

The visit went well, Puckles got her container of chicken puff snacks, and off we went to continue our routine – until the phone rang. It was my cousin, calling to tell me that someone had dropped off a pathetic looking small black and white Shih Tzu at my vet's office. Her granddaughter, who worked for our vet, had taken the dog to her house, hoping to find him a home.

Imagine they thought of me, the person who was banned by her husband from going to animal rescues. I am not allowed to visit rescue centers because Walt has this notion that I would bring them all home with me. Well, we have fostered quite a few dogs and a few cats through the years. It's those pleading eyes!

Well, banned I was, until I got that call. How could I say no?

Off I went to see this little guy. I told myself he would probably need lots of medical care and it didn't really sound like he was going to be a match for our home anyway. That all changed as soon as I saw him. My heart broke for him. It was apparent that he had been so neglected it was shocking. He had already been bathed three times, yet was still a true mess. The stench that permeated his entire body made the room stink like a very disgusting outhouse. It was a smell I will not soon forget.

Were it not for the mass of matted hair all over his head and body, you could count his ribs. The hair was especially matted around his eyes and there was substantial drainage from them, both dried and fresh. One eye looked like his vision was either gone or close to being gone. Quite a few teeth were missing from his little mouth. His self-esteem and trust level were as poor as his physical condition; he would not give eye contact and he kept his head down. Still, I could literally feel his pain and knew we needed each other.

I called Walt and explained how badly this little guy needed us. He didn't sound too enthusiastic, but allowed me to bring him home. There was one condition, however. I would bring this nervous, pathetic boy home with the agreement that he would be returned and found a new home if it didn't work out. The truth is that I couldn't imagine ever giving him back, despite having no idea of his health condition or how he would look. All I knew was that I had to give him a good home with lots of love because he so needed it.

Walt was pretty shocked when I presented him with

my newest rescue because I had played down his condition during our phone conversation. He wondered if he could possibly clean up. There wasn't much weight to him and his little bones rubbed with the slightest movement. His matted hair was overgrown and his eyes were so matted and crusted. We could not even imagine what he had endured in his life before finding us.

My job was to try to get the mats out without hurting or scaring him. This turned out to be no easy task. I was so fearful of cutting him. I put him in the tub and spent a long time working on him. I think he was eager to be cleaned up, too. Through it all, he was so patient. Once he was clean enough to come out of the bathtub, it was time to get the bigger mats out.

Luckily, our groomer worked him in the very next day. She had no choice but to shave him right down to his skin. Oh my! He just stood there shivering, looking even more pathetic and emaciated than ever. At least he was clean and no longer smelled like sewage. As I saw him there, still avoiding eye contact, thoughts of the neglect and possible abuse he endured broke my heart. It made me even more determined to make him feel loved and safe.

· · ·

I am a Reiki practitioner, which is a method of touch healing that helps to balance energy within. In doing so, symptoms on various levels–mind, body and spirit are often eased, including pain. I began giving him Reiki daily. I could sense the intense heat in his hip joints and lower back. He responded well to the treatments and my reassurances of love and safety right from the start. His little body would relax under my hands as it drew in energy. Still, it was virtually months before he would let us hold him for long, and even longer before he would look at us. He insisted on having his body positioned so that his head faced away from us.

Gradually, our little boy transformed. He has settled in quite nicely and no longer resembles the scared little boy who came to our home over a year ago. He continues enjoying his treatments, only now he even enjoys having me touch his tummy. Sometimes, he drifts to sleep with his head hanging off my lap.

Juju, who we named after our then eleven year old grandson Julian, is now a happy, playful dog. The name just seemed to fit, and when I sent his picture to Julian he was excited. When they met for the first time, it was as though they had always known each other. We had to watch them closely because there was talk of stealing him and taking him back to Boston!

Juju loves his home so well that, true to his Shih Tzu nature, he has become very protective. He is quite selective of who may enter. We had not seen that side of him until a doctor friend brought a gentleman from New York City to my home for a Reiki session. Juju made no sound at all and gave no warning. He just went right for the man's ankle. Not exactly a warm welcome, but luckily there was no damage done.

We were shocked by his behavior and had no idea what triggered him. Was it a body scent? Size? A way of moving? Tone of voice? Only Juju knows. Occasionally, repair people coming to the house trigger the same response. It's interesting because he does go right up to some men in a friendly manner.

Juju has a special attachment to my husband. He loves to sit with him in his easy chair and watch TV. Sometimes he climbs up on his chest and stares into his eyes for a long time. We are convinced he is telling him how happy he is and how much he loves him. Now didn't that just put a smile on your face?

Walt was a professional firefighter until 1990 when he was injured in an arson fire. His injuries included some brain damage from anoxia, resulting in numerous neurological deficits. He was prescribed an incredible amount of prescriptions and often suffered from depression. Miss Puckles and Reiki are what saved him. He bonded with her quickly because of the unconditional love she gave him. She gave him a reason to get out of bed. Puckles was our first animal to bond with him. Then Juju entered the picture and they have a special connection also.

. . .

Were you wondering how Juju got along with Miss Puckles, the queen of her domain? They had to do the dance and get used to their smells. Juju was obsessed with her and even tried to mate with her. We corrected that behavior quickly, and none too soon for her.

Puckles mistakenly thought he was brought home for the sole purpose of being her playmate. He was not having that at all. He would freeze with his head down whenever she wanted to play. Poor Puckles would look at me with a puzzled expression on her face. It was like she was trying to figure out why he wouldn't play and what was wrong with him. She was quite sad about it. Like his other trusting issues, this took time.

Today, Juju and Puckles are best friends. I must admit she does get a little jealous when he reigns in her daddy's chair. They sometimes both think they are alpha dogs, and one almost climbs to his head to show rank. Now that is funny!

. . .

I sense that wherever Juju was, his trust issues may have involved females. He was longer in trusting me, which is so out of the ordinary. My friends often refer to me as the animal whisperer because most animals connect with me immediately. Juju's reticence was difficult for me. Even so, I always respected his boundaries and never tried to force him to do anything that felt threatening to him.

Now Juju loves me and looks at me as his playmate. He loves to run and jump and play like a puppy. He especially likes squeaky toys. I am expected to get down on the floor and play with him and his toys, especially in the morning and after dinner. I am also the one who feeds him, cleans his eyes, and when needed, give baths and medicine. He has such trust now and never fusses. He is sleeping under my desk right now as I type this. I think he is worn out from his play.

Still, when my husband and I sit side by side, there is no question where the dogs sit. Juju sits next to Walt and Puckles hugs my leg. It's almost as though they have this unwritten agreement—I belong to her and he belongs to Walter. Sometimes, when they are together on the bed, Puckles wants to get close too. Juju will either body check her or go at her in attack mode. He never really attacks, but is convincing enough that our twenty-pound darling backs off.

Those rare nights when Puckles is in another room and Juju wants to be in my lap are very special to me. He has been known to climb up and look me right in the eyes. The first time he did it I felt such overwhelming love. There is just something about that little face that makes my heart so joyful.

We cherish every day that we have with Juju. He is a breath of fresh air. He makes us laugh even when things are a little rough. Being a part of Juju's transformation and sharing a bond of unconditional love with him makes our hearts sing with joy. If you are an animal lover, you know what I mean. It's as if he radiates a light like that from the sun. The funny thing is, just being in his presence sparks that feeling. He and his side kick put it all into perspective for us—to be happy and enjoy this very moment in life.

We cannot imagine life without our Juju.

Story by Sandra Smith

EPILOGUE

I wish we could say that Juju's story had a happily ever after ending, at least as far as happily ever after goes in dog years, but a few weeks after Sandi submitted her story, less than two years after he was rescued, Juju's health took a turn for the worse. It appears that he had an adult onset genetic condition of his esophagus which led to pneumonia and health problems he could not recover from. Despite their best efforts to help him, Juju's condition would not turn around and Sandi and Walt had to make the heart-wrenching decision to end his suffering.

When you have hearts as big as Sandi and Walt, however, that is not the end of the story. Soon after Juju's death, Sandi got a call about Leonardo (Leo), a much loved Schnauzer needing to be re-homed because of his owner's health problems. Leo and Miss Puckles quickly became friends and he is now a member of the family. A few months later, Sandi fell in love with Julie and Peanut, two pups through Paws Across Oswego County. Leo, Julie and Peanut will never replace Juju in their hearts, but as many dog parents know, when you lose a dog and your heart breaks, it breaks open even wider to let new love in.

Walt, Julie, Peanut and Sandi

I do not concern myself with my inability to feel such comfort amidst humans (other than with very few friends and family), but, rather, am simply thankful that at least dogs exist, and I'm humbly aware of how much less a person I'd be—how less a human—if they did not exist.

~Rick Bass, *Colter: The True Story of the Best Dog I Ever Had*

FROM FOSTER TO FOREVER

Teddy joined us as an unexpected but much wanted guest on a sunny Friday afternoon in May of 2012. Only three days before, I had tentatively broached the subject of fostering a small adult dog from the shelter with my husband, Scott. It had been less than two months since losing Louis, my beloved French Bulldog, and I wasn't ready to open my heart or home to another lifelong canine companion.

Even so, I couldn't stay away. Weeks of looking on petfinder.com made me painfully aware of how many homeless dogs were in need love and care. Fostering seemed the perfect way to lend a hand and satisfy my yearning for a dog without emotional and long term ties.

Scott was concerned that I would want to keep our foster dogs, but I knew I would be alright with it. My parents had owned a boarding kennel and we raised dogs for years, so I was no stranger to dogs coming and going. The hardest part was thinking they might feel abandoned while they were back at the shelter waiting for a home. I reasoned with myself that this was not a valid worry because around here smaller dogs usually get adopted within days. Besides, what could be more rewarding than helping them get ready for a second chance at a good life?

Since I have my summers free, that seemed an ideal time to start. I would have plenty of time to nurture a dog or two and even do some training to make them more adoptable. Part of me had a strong urge to procrastinate about following through with this decision, but a more powerful compulsion to get my paper work done right away had me driving straight to the SPCA of Jefferson County after work on Thursday. When I got there they were quite busy; volunteers were being trained and a little dog (who I could not see) was waiting in a covered crate for his foster people. I was told it would be a few weeks before my home check and approval were finalized.

It didn't take that long.

. . .

When I arrived home after work the next day, the blinking light of the answering machine greeted me. "We have a little dog here that needs medical care. Can you take him for a week or so?" I quickly called my husband, and with his blessing and a bit of trepidation, I headed for the shelter.

As they lifted the towels covering his crate, I got my first look at our foster boy. Despite his new haircut and adorable cuteness, it was obvious that Teddy had been traumatized. His body trembled and his eyes had that sad, glassy look. His once long curly hair was clipped very short and his rear was shaved.

"Put this cream on his hind end twice a day. Keep it clean. He may be able to stand for a few seconds if you help him get up."

"What's his story?" I asked.

Thanks to the microchip embedded under his skin, they were able to get some information about him. His original owner said he was a two year old Teddy Bear (usually a mix between a Bichon Frisé and a Shih Tzu). He lived with them for a year and a half before being given to a second owner six months prior to his rescue. He must have either escaped from that place, or was dumped to walk the local army base alone. He was found filthy and matted. The big mats on his behind were encrusted with feces and maggots; they were so tight to his skin that he could not fully pass his stools. What couldn't come out backed up, which caused great pain and poor anal tone. He was at risk of becoming incontinent if the damage didn't heal.

As soon as we got home, I carefully took Teddy from the crate and carried him to a tree. I helped him stand up, but within a few seconds he sat down and peed, getting it all over his legs and feet. "No worries, little guy," I said. "I'll wash you up in the sink."

After a quick wash and a long drink of water, we left him to rest in the crate. The scenario repeated itself a few hours later. He refused to eat, except for a tiny piece of chicken.

My husband, the one who was worried I would get too attached if we fostered, was instantly taken with Teddy. Before the sun had even set I heard these foretelling words, "Come to Daddy."

Of course, Teddy didn't come. Teddy couldn't walk.

Around eight o'clock that evening, I carried Teddy onto my bed. I didn't know how he would react, or if he would even want to be petted, but I felt like I had to try something to help him feel better. He rested on the bed pad near me without complaint, and soon dozed off to soft words and gentle strokes. He did not make a sound or move for almost two hours, with the exception of a barely perceptible sigh about forty-five minutes before he woke up. Little did I know the meaning of that sigh–until we made one last trip outdoors.

Just like before, I carefully set him down by the tree. Only this time, instead of sitting there, he stood right up and tootled a few yards over to another tree. What a shock! Now it was my turn to feel scared – that he would run off in the dark. Thankfully, he came back as soon as I called his name.

As soon as we got back in the house, there was no doubt that a miraculous transformation had taken place on that bed. Scott and I stared at Teddy in disbelief as he sat on the kitchen floor looking at us with head up, tail wagging and eyes shining. I swear he was smiling. He gladly accepted each bit of kibble as though it were a piece of steak. It was like he was a new dog.

I make a practice of meditating on situations, especially difficult ones, to find meaning and life lessons that will help me evolve as a person. There in front of me was my little visitor, offering the perfect opportunity to learn from him right then. While watching him in those moments, I marveled at how powerful and transformative the spirit is in healing. I am familiar with the mind body connection and the ability of the mind to heal. I study and write about it, and have experienced it for myself. It was how instantaneous and effortlessly it happened for Teddy that took me by surprise. You would have to see the incredible difference in his affect and behavior to believe such a change could take place so quickly. His resilience awed, inspired and challenged my beliefs and assumptions about what we need to heal. How could he release his emotional pain so quickly, and open himself so readily to love and trust after all he had been through? What a profound lesson this little gray and white dog was teaching us without saying a word.

We had all assumed Teddy was physically incapable of standing and walking because of his physical condition, yet what we witnessed that night told a very different story. It turned out he could not only stand, but could easily jump on the furniture and take short walks. In reality, he must have been so disheartened and emotionally wounded that he had no will to stand. When he felt safe and loved, his renewed spirit brought with it the will to live and be happy again, and his body responded. *"How true that must be for each of us,"* I thought.

Love truly is the great healer.

. . .

It would be wonderful to say that Teddy was all better after that. He wasn't. His reddened skin and damaged colon took weeks to heal. Although he was not incontinent, defecating was very challenging for him. He whimpered, cried out in pain, and licked at himself every time he passed his very thin, poorly formed stools. It broke my heart to watch him go through that.

As the days went by, it became obvious that Teddy's suffering was not limited to physical neglect. The first time Scott scolded him for raiding tissues from the trash can, he ran out of the room with his body pressed up against the wall. Brooms and big black garbage bags terrified him; no matter how much I coaxed, he refused to get near them. For months, he ravenously wolfed every morsel of kibble in his bowl, and he was obsessed with scavenging for anything and everything he considered edible, some of which was rather nasty. "Who could have done this to such a sweet dog?" we repeatedly asked.

Despite these issues, Teddy has proven to be a happy, obedient, lively dog with a joy for life and a love for dogs and people. He is very friendly and tries to get every dog he meets, big or small, to play with him. He has a protective side, too. Within three days of adopting us and making our house his home, he appointed himself guardian of the turf. We often find him on his perch atop the couch keeping watch at the window overlooking the driveway. No deer, rabbit, bird, or unfamiliar dog better dare enter his yard! Only his best friends, Bentley the Golden Retriever and Toby the Boxer, are welcomed enthusiastically.

From day one, Teddy (almost) always came when called. No matter what smells are enthralling him in the yard, he runs full speed at the sound of his name, knowing a swift return is rewarded with a treat. He rewards us for coming home, too, by whining and barking excitedly at the window before running around the house, quivering and jumping with excitement. Knowing the doggy in the window is awaiting my return makes me step just a little harder on the gas pedal on my way home from work. Sometimes I come home to find my shoe, never chewed, keeping him company.

. . .

Teddy became an official family member two weeks after arriving as our guest. He and my husband had that decision made on day one. Scott's mother, who also adores Teddy and has him visit often, cast her vote, too. My niece affectionately dubbed us foster failures. I call us an adoption success story.

I have been reminded through my fostering experience with Teddy that some wisdom is only gained in hindsight. Sometimes, looking back is the only way to see a divine plan transpiring in our lives. I believe forces greater than us were at play to make this adoption happen. Was it a coincidence that Teddy came to us on May 11th, my parents' 67th and final wedding anniversary? I wish I had asked, but I truly believe he was in the covered crate waiting for foster parents who never came, and that's why they called me early the next morning. Why else would I have felt so compelled to rush to the shelter when summer vacation was still six weeks away?

As I look back, I clearly see that Teddy was meant to join our family that very day. If I had waited much longer to begin the process, my plans to foster would have been thwarted. Worse than that, Teddy would not have been there to make what life was bringing my way more bearable.

By the first week of July, my worsening back

symptoms turned into unrelenting pain from a ruptured disk. As I moved around the house trying to find a way to stop the pain, Teddy rarely left my side. His presence comforted me, and he even gave up his cozy spot on the bed to lie beside me on the floor. This went on for several days until I had surgery. Less than a week later, my mother died.

Through it all, Teddy was there for me like only a dog could be. His antics brought smiles to our faces during that sad time, and he never let me miss a daily therapy walk during my recovery, even when I didn't feel like going. I could not imagine enduring that back ordeal and losing Lou and my mother within such a short time without a canine companion.

Dogs are masters of creating emotionally safe space just by being themselves. This is very difficult to put into words, but it is as if something deep within our souls resonates with their energy, their unwavering unconditional love and unbridled joy to be in our presence, their undivided loyalty, and complete trust in us. Dogs make us feel special, and teach us by example to relish simple pleasures and live totally in the moment. They teach us there is only now and only who you are, who you are with, and what you are doing right then–and what could be better than to sniff the wind and be in the company of those you love?

. . .

It may be true that we rescued Teddy, but as is so often the case, he rescued us, too. Every day he brings life and happiness to our home (and some occasional mischief!). His body is fully healed and his emotions are healing. I love hearing him make happy growling noises when he plays now instead of being silent, and that he finally puts up a fight in a game of tug-o-war. He no longer shirks at the sight of the broom or slinks along the walls when scolded. He has begun to cozy up with me during loud storms instead of seeking refuge under the bed, and sometimes he lets me hold him while he sleeps, which shows me he is at ease with us, and that makes me feel good.

We have had Teddy over a year now, and even though he gives us plenty to chat about, our favorite topic is still the 'magic bed' and how quickly his spirit healed in the presence of love. That is a lesson of hope for all who are and have been emotionally wounded. It is a lesson we will long remember and embrace.

Story by Val Silver

I think dogs are the most amazing creatures;
they give unconditional love. For me they are the
role model for being alive.

~Gilda Radner

Photo of Val Silver and Teddy

BISCUIT THE DO-OVER DOG

Sometimes, shelter and rescue dogs take the short road from one family to another. Other times, their journeys are longer and more involved. Just like people who cannot bounce back quickly from injury, abuse, or neglect without an extra dose of love and time to heal, some dogs also need support to become their best selves again.

Biscuit was one of those dogs. Although she was in desperate need of help from people, she was the dog no one wanted. Her story, as we first knew it, began when she was dropped off in a gassing facility with three strikes against her. She had a fracture to her right front leg, which made her elbow fully detach. She was in a lot of pain and had difficulty walking. The family who found her and brought her in stated that she was child and dog aggressive. To make matters worse, Biscuit was mislabeled as a pit bull mix at the shelter. This practically sealed her fate, because of their policy to not adopt out pit bulls. The future did not look bright for this death row dog.

Fortunately for Biscuit, two women, Susan and Cheryl, saw her story on the shelter's Facebook page and became her rescue angels. Even though they lived several states away, they rallied behind her and networked with others to find a good rescue group for her. Thanks to their efforts, donations by people who cared, and Heart to Heart Rescue, Biscuit was saved from an almost certain death, and given a second chance for a better life.

This is Biscuit's original picture when we were asked to help her. She had donations, but most orthopedic vets were quoting $3000 to fix her leg. We knew our vet would do it for a lot less so we took a chance on her.

· · ·

The first leg of Biscuit's journey to her new life began with her rescue. From the shelter, she was taken to the airfield where she boarded a 1978 Piper Warrior plane owned by Pilots N Paws volunteer Andy Mckevitz, for her flight from Henderson, North Carolina to Knoxville, Tennessee. In Knoxville, she was handed off to Lee Hitchens for an overnight stay. Then she was transported another 250 miles by several more volunteers each driving a 60-90 mile leg of her journey until she reached her destination-the vet's office in Louisville, Kentucky.

. . .

After a successful surgery, Biscuit still had a long painful road of healing ahead of her. Because her elbow was completely detached, she needed internal and external pins. She had a four week stay at the clinic, followed by two weeks of foster care; the whole time she was confined to a crate except for bathroom breaks, and then back to the vet for another two plus weeks of crate rest after the external apparatus was removed. This was followed by weeks at my home for foster care and physical therapy including gentle walking, moving the muscle manually, and taking her to the pool to rebuild her atrophied shoulder muscles. The vet estimated that she had been at least three months without use of her leg before her surgery.

. . .

During the time Biscuit was healing physically, her behavior wasn't improving much. She was standoffish and fear aggressive, especially around unfamiliar dogs and men. She would growl and bark at them until she got to know them. Obviously, she needed to improve her behavior, as it did not make her a good candidate for adoption.

In order to help her heal emotionally and address her

issues, Biscuit would have to work with our trainer. The plan was for Tammy to keep her for six weeks to teach her basic commands and good citizenship. She would take her to the stores and everywhere she went for exposure to people and different situations.

When we arrived at Tammy's house, she looked at me as though I had three heads. I couldn't figure out why; she knew we were coming and I had already told her about the dog. Well, it turns out that she knew Biscuit, and had trained her once before. Biscuit's previous owner, a German man, had brought her to Tammy for training as a protection dog for his business (even though that didn't fit her true personality). Sometime after her training, they moved from Kentucky to North Carolina. It wasn't long after that Biscuit ended up as a stray. Sure enough, she obeyed commands in German and answered to her previous name, Sasha.

Still, this didn't change the fact that Biscuit needed help for her behavioral issues. During her stay, Tammy, a highly skilled service dog trainer, realized that she had the aptitude to become a service dog because she alerted to things. We decided to move forward with that training to make her more adoptable. The first step was to find the right match for her because service dogs are trained specifically to meet their owner's needs. Biscuit also had to be matched with someone who would not require her to walk a lot.

When the match was made, she was fully trained as a PTSD and Diabetic Alert dog for a woman who recently lost her canine helper. Unfortunately, when the time came for Biscuit to go home, the woman's medical issues made it impossible for her to take her.

We found another match for Biscuit, and she was

retrained as a therapy assistant for a small boy with ADHD and other concerns. She now lives in Louisville, Kentucky with her new family.

. . .

Biscuit's do-over story is personal to her, yet she also represents many dogs like her who need rescuing the most. They may not always be the most sought after breeds or the easiest cases medically or behaviorally, but that is what rescue is about-giving a second chance to dogs that really need us.

Biscuit was transformed from a sad, fear aggressive death row dog with a painful injury no one was taking care of, to a well adjusted, fully trained service dog ready and willing to love and help a child have a better life-all because a group of human angels saw her need and her heart, and cared enough to help.

Oh, and what kind of dog is Biscuit? She may appear to be a rather ordinary looking mix, but she is actually a very rare breed of dog. She is a Carolina dog, or American Dingo, a highly intelligent breed of primitive dogs believed to be direct descendants of the ancient pariah dogs that crossed the Bering Strait over 8,000 years ago.

Story by Kim Massey as told to Val Silver
Audio interview available

God requires that we assist the animals, when they need our help. Each being (human or creature) has the same right of protection.

~St. Francis of Assisi

Perhaps the human condition will always include attempts to remind ourselves that we are separate from the rest of the natural world. We are different from other animals; it's undeniably true. But while acknowledging that, we must acknowledge another truth, the truth that we are also the same. That is what dogs and their emotions give us—a connection. A connection to life on earth, to all that binds and cradles us, lest we begin to feel too alone. Dogs are our bridge—our connection to who we really are, and most tellingly, who we want to be.

~Patricia B. McConnell, *For the Love of a Dog: Understanding Emotion in You and Your Best Friend*

RESCUE ME SENIORS

Senior dogs make wonderful pets, and are so grateful for a second chance to give and get love, yet like other 'undesirables'–big dogs, black dogs, and dogs with special needs–it is often more difficult for them to find good homes.

Just as for humans, there is no magic number that turns a canine into a senior. A good rule of thumb is that the bigger the dog, the shorter the life span. Big dogs enter their golden years at six to eight years of age, while smaller dogs with 14-17 year life spans may not be considered seniors until they are eight to ten years old.

There are many good reasons to adopt a senior dog. They are less energetic than youngsters, are likely to be housebroken, and are less likely to chew your belongings. They make wonderful companions for mature and less active owners. Contrary to opinion, seniors do bond with their new families and often settle in easily. Adopting a senior gives you the opportunity to provide a much appreciated home for a needy dog. You will truly change a life forever, and as you will see in the *Rescue Me Seniors* stories, your new family member can change your life for the better, too.

. . .

The following stories tell of four dog lovers who opened their hearts and homes to older dogs in need, how their dogs blessed their lives in return, and why they wouldn't have it any other way.

HAPPINESS IS A SENIOR DOG

When MJ, my yellow lab, died at nine years old of bone cancer, I was heartbroken. He was that one dog in a million. I could not imagine another dog ever measuring up to him, so in my grief I decided to never get another. I gathered up all his stuff and donated it the local humane society. They got a lot of stuff because he was one spoiled dog with lots of toys.

It felt so lonely without a dog. I missed MJ so much that I went into a deep depression. My cat PS was also mourning her close friend, so I adopted another cat with the feline immunodeficiency virus (FIV) to keep her company.

Back then, I was working as an 18 wheeler truck driver for a local company. Several times a day I had pickups at a place right behind the Norfolk SPCA. I would cry as I saw the dogs getting their outdoor exercise. Then I would go home and torture myself and cry some more by looking at different dogs for adoption on-line. Still, I would tell myself, "NO."

That is, until I saw Winnie-the-Pooh at a small local no-kill shelter, Animal Resources of Tidewater. Due to unforeseen circumstances, she lost her home of seven years. My heart went out to her. I thought, "I lost my dog son and she lost her momma. We will heal each other." In honor and memory of MJ, I had decided that I would only adopt older animals because they were the ones who need it the most and are chosen the least. At seven years old and homeless, Winnie fit the bill on both counts.

Once approved for adoption, I was invited to meet Winnie. She surprised me! I was expecting a slower moving dog, but she was a ball of energy. We don't have a fenced yard, but I knew I could handle her. I was sold when I sat on the floor and she started licking my face.

Before she could come home, there was one more step. I had to pass the 'Gracie test'. Gracie is a very intuitive dog owned by Winnie's foster mom, Elaine. She uses this dog to 'vet' people. Once it was clear that Gracie liked me, Winnie was mine.

Our first day together

. . .

Winnie and I bonded and I fell in love with her. At first I felt guilty for loving another dog, but I knew that if something had happened to me I would have wanted MJ to be loved by someone else. I began to feel so much better and happier once I had a dog again. I couldn't wait to get home from work every day to see my wiggling bundle of joy.

Over time, Elaine and I became friends and she told me some very interesting things about Winnie. She had fostered Winnie's mother along with her 11 puppies from the time they were three days old until they were adopted out at eight weeks old. She had fostered Winnie as a pup and she got her start through ART!

That turned out to be a very lucky twist of fate for Winnie. ART requires adopters to sign a waiver agreeing to return the dog to them should they ever choose to give it up. For some reason, Winnie's owner surrendered her to one of the areas highest-kill shelters instead. Thankfully, Winnie had on her rabies tag. When the shelter called the vet to learn her medical history, he remembered which organization she came from. He knew Winnie because her former owner had worked at his office and brought her to work every day. ART pulled Winnie out of there the very next day and she went back to Elaine for fostering again.

Because Elaine keeps in touch with the owners of a few of Winnie's siblings, I have also gotten to know two of her sisters. The dogs play together and I even dog sit for one of them sometimes. One of the owners did a DNA test and found out the girls are three-quarters pit bull and one-fourth Italian greyhound. You can see these breeds in Winnie. She has the big chest and the wide head of a pit bull and her body tapers down to a real scrawny backside. Her feet, legs and toes are extra long and skinny. When she sits down her feet are too long and they stick up in the air. She is so funny looking.

Winnie will be eleven years old on December 4th and is still an energetic girl. She just had blood work done and it was perfect. The vet said if she didn't know her age, she'd think she was three or four years old. She still loves to chase squirrels and runs like a pup. Now that I'm disabled and often in pain, I can't exercise her like she'd like, so we wait until dark to go outside and I shine the laser light for her to run after. She chases it just like the cats do! I have good voice control over her so I don't worry about her leaving the yard. Sometimes she runs around the house just for the pure joy of it. She wiggles and comes up to me. I say, "Run, Little Winnie" and off she goes for another circuit.

Winnie is a happy dog and she makes me feel happy. That is my story of my little Winnie.

. . .

For a few years, we just had Winnie and the two cats. Then I met Sammy...

ME AND MY SHADOW

After getting laid off from my job as a truck driver, I started doing a little volunteer work at our local low kill shelter, the Portsmouth Humane Society. Like so many rescues and shelters, they rely heavily on donations to make ends meet and volunteers to care for and train their animals.

As my arthritis got progressively worse, I would go down there once in a while, but eventually even just sitting on the floor playing with the cats became too painful. One way I still help out is to foster animals and to provide for their needs while I have them to save the shelter some money.

In May of 2012, I was at the shelter giving my friends a tour of the new building with indoor/outdoor kennels. As we walked around greeting the dogs, I saw a new sign that said 'Sammy, Golden Retriever Mix, 12 years old, Owner surrender. I peeked in and called to him. He stuck his little nose out. I called again, "Sammy, come here sweetheart." What I saw when he came outside shocked me. The front half of his body looked fine, but from the shoulders back he was totally bald, right down to the end of his skinny tail. His body was covered with scabs and pussy, nasty sores. He was trembling with fear as he looked up at me with his big, sad eyes. I spoke to him and he wagged his tail a little, and trembled some more.

I turned right around, went to the adoption counselor's desk, and said I wanted to take Sammy home as a foster. She said it was going to be for hospice because he was very sick, very old, and they did not have enough money to spend on an old dog when so many young dogs were also in need.

I learned that the owners surrendering him said he was ten years old, too sick to live, and wanted him put to sleep. They had not taken him to a vet to find out what was wrong, and would not take him to a vet to be euthanized. Even though it was explained to them that things didn't happen that way, and it would be less traumatic for Sammy to go to the vet, they said no. They wanted to just pay the small shelter fee and be rid of him. They knew he would be evaluated, saved if possible, and would possibly live out his last days in terror. Seniors tend to me even more afraid when entering the shelter than young dogs, and are often terrified.

Sam was quarantined for three weeks before joining the general population. The vet who volunteers at the shelter estimated that he was 12 years old, and diagnosed him with several bacterial and yeast infections that affected most of his skin. He was also chewing skin off his front feet. He was on three different antibiotics, an antidepressant to help with the chewing OCD and fear. He was underweight because he wasn't eating.

I said okay, I still wanted him. At least he would spend

his last days knowing he was loved. Before I could take him home, Sam and Winnie had to decide if they liked each other. In his evaluation, Sam showed that he was selective, meaning he accepts some dogs and not others. Fortunately, he and Winnie got along fine. He jumped in the van like he was saying "Yay, I'm outa' here."

He was less sure about what to do when we got to the house. He looked at me; he looked at the house, then back at me again. I encouraged him to come in. Finally, he wagged his tail and headed off to explore. He had the same hesitancy about the couch. It took him a while to understand he was allowed up there. In the meantime, he would not get on it if we were around, but sometimes we would find him there when we got home. He didn't want to get caught, and would jump right off!

. . .

I wanted to help Sammy heal, so I did some research. I started adding yogurt, ground flax, fish oil, and other supplements for arthritis and skin to his food. I learned that chamomile tea was very good for sores on dogs, so I fed that to him and sponged it on his skin.

Sammy's skin was not his only problem. When he went to the bathroom in our yard, I looked and wondered, "Is his poop moving?" I scooped some up and ran it to the vet to see what it was. Sammy had so many tape worms that he was pooping them out. After his first dose of medicine he made a huge bowel movement of nothing but worms. It looked like a bowl full of long fettuccine and they were flat and ruffled like lasagna noodles. I did not want to clean that up but I had to, so on went the rubber gloves. *"Eew, how do I do this?"*

Soon after that, Sammy started getting better and began playing with toys. Within a few weeks he had tufts of hair growing – the vet could not believe her eyes. She asked, "What have you been doing to this dog?" and encouraged me to keep it up. Within a year this once bald momma's boy had to be shaved down because he had so much hair he was getting too hot. He is not under hospice care anymore. That is a miracle, a real success story.

After Sammy was well, he had two potential adopters. I spoke with the first one on the phone. He wanted an old dog who would just lay there while his two toddlers crawled on him. I said, "Mister, this is an old, arthritic dog, and he would be in pain and might bite your children to protect himself." He got my point.

In October, someone else was interested and the shelter called to see when I could bring him down to meet them. That is when I realized I couldn't let this boy go. I adopted him on a wing and a prayer. I had no idea how I was going to care for this dog. I had not yet been approved for disability because of the arthritis, and had little money and no insurance. I was living alone on my small savings and a charge card. Still, I knew this dog needed to stay with me. I prayed for God to help me and somehow we managed. I was approved in November and my disability check arrived ten days later (instead of the usual 8-12 weeks.)

. . .

Like anyone, human or dog, Sammy is not without his quirks and foibles. From the very get-go Sammy would not let me out of his sight. He won't eat unless I am standing beside him, and if I leave he follows me. Because he sleeps more soundly and is a little deafer, he doesn't always realize right away that I left the room. But it's like he has a sixth sense about it. Usually it doesn't take too long for me to hear that huffing and puffing as he scurries around the house looking for me so he can get close again. I always sing, *"Me and my shadow, do-do-do-do, me and my shadow..."* to him, the same song I used to hear my mother sing.

Sammy throws temper tantrums, too, but rarely barks. When a cat is on one of the many beds in the house, and he wants that bed, he huffs and puffs and stamps his front feet. Of course, he always wants the bed the cat has. He is also a bit of a night owl. Around 3 AM, he gets up from the twin mattress he sleeps on beside my bed. I'll hear him huffing and puffing, pretending to have to go to the bathroom. Most of the time what he really wants is 'me-time' alone with momma. We play a bit in the living room and then go back to bed.

The vet and I believe that in addition to being neglected medically, Sammy may have been abused, which explains why he's so quiet. He finally started barking after he was more relaxed, but it was the strangest, most high pitched bark I ever heard. I started calling him "Squeakers". It may also explain why he flinches and growls when you startle him or speak sternly to him. One day, when he growled and bared his teeth at another dog, I scolded, "Sam, No." He went into a crouch, started shaking, and snarled at me. I was so surprised. When I comfort him, he relaxes and quits.

. . .

I helped heal Sam physically, and continue to help him heal emotionally. He has been good for me, too. My dogs are always there for me, and are natural empaths. When I am having a panic attack, Winnie senses it right away. She jumps up, crawls in my lap and cuddles. I put my arms around her and talk to her. She takes my mind off it and I calm down. Sam constantly wanting to follow me shows just how much he loves me and how grateful he feels. It makes me feel so good to know I can give them the love they deserve. When I wake up in the morning, there they are looking at me with love in their eyes, tails wagging. What better way to start my days, looking into their eyes with one hand on each of them.

. . .

I have learned that there are different types of love, and we may have many people we love, but no love is as pure as an animal's love. They are so dedicated and accepting, they are always there for me. My dogs complete me. The fact that I can give back a little bit by fostering and adopting and providing for their needs makes me feel great. It warms my heart.

There is a mistaken belief that older dogs won't bond with you because they are used to someone else. That is not true. Look at my two. Sammy was my shadow from the beginning. He knew I saved his life.

I say, "Do it." I believe you get more satisfaction from adopting older dogs. You know what you are getting. They are usually housebroken and less energetic which is especially good for somebody who can't be dragged around the block because it hurts too much. And they are just so grateful. They know that they have been given a second chance or a third chance. They know and they are wonderful.

I'm a senior citizen. I'm 55 years old and disabled. I'd hate to think that someone would euthanize me because I'm having trouble walking. It's no different for them. Give senior dogs or cats a place in your heart and home and they will thank you with their love and loyalty for the rest of their lives.

Stories by Letha Hundley as told to Val Silver
Audio interview available on the webpage

The one absolutely unselfish friend that man can have in this selfish world, the one that never deserts him, the one that never proves ungrateful or treacherous, is his dog. ... He will kiss the hand that has no food to offer; he will lick the wounds and sores that come in encounter with the roughness of the world. ... When all other friends desert, he remains.

~George G. Vest, U.S. Senate speech, 1884

A DOG OF MY OWN TO LOVE

When my children, Shawn and Rhiannon, were growing up we were a very close knit family that always had several pets because we all loved animals so much. There were dogs, cats, guinea pigs, hamsters, birds and fish. We took great care of them and shared the duties equally.

Shawn was 18 when he left home to join the Army's 82nd Airborne Division. He is eight years older than his sister, so my nest wasn't totally empty yet. That changed when Rhiannon was 17. She finished high school a year early because she was homeschooled, and left home to dance professionally.

I was alright with this until my kitty passed away from cancer a few years ago. I am a caretaker by nature, and felt an empty spot inside me. Even though our children have since married, moved close by, and blessed us with grandchildren we see and babysit for often, I missed having pets. They are my babies, and I so wanted a furry little soul of my own to nurture and care for.

My prayer was answered in January, 2012. My

daughter-in-law thought I wanted a puppy, so she sent me sent me a bunch of puppy pictures on Facebook from the Portsmouth Humane Society. They were promoting their Puppy Palooza, a special adoption event for adoptable adults and puppies, being held that weekend. Among the puppy photos was a photo of an eight year old French Bulldog named Hess who caught my attention. It was important to me that I adopt a dog in need of a home. A lot of people don't want senior dogs, they want puppies. I thought if I could give a senior dog a home even for a few years that would be great.

That Saturday, I went to see him, and stayed for about an hour and a half just holding him and talking to him. He was so gentle and loving. His foster mother Tiffany told me that Hess was found walking the road by himself in the cold of mid-December. No one knew why or how he got there. He is such a sweet boy that I can only imagine and hope it was because he got lost somehow. I imagined how much his owners were missing him.

She explained that by the time he was picked up and brought to the shelter, he was in pitiful condition. He was very sick and almost starved to death. He had a cough, watery nasal discharge, was retching and had a slight fever. The vet diagnosed him with kennel cough and severe malnutrition. Kennel cough, is a highly contagious viral infection that affects the respiratory system. Tiffany nursed him back to health with antibiotics, lots of rest, and a healthy diet for six weeks before she felt he was ready for adoption. He was still in her care when she brought him to the Puppy Palooza. Hess was so underweight that even after six weeks of care he only weighed 13 pounds.

Normally, they make you wait 24 hours before taking a

dog, but they saw how good we were together and that I really cared about him, so they said would let me take him home that day. I went outside to call my husband Brian, and cried for joy when he said yes, I could have him. I was so happy.

. . .

We named our little boy Yoda because he is old and wise, just like his namesake. He also looks like Yoda from Star Wars when you put the brown throw over him to look like a robe. The morning I took this picture I was playing with him. He looked so cute!

Yoda fully recovered and now weighs in at a healthy 20 pounds. He does have a few minor health problems that have nothing to do with his ordeal. He has allergies and sneezes a lot, so the vet has him on antihistamines. He also enlarged one of the disks in his back, which caused nerve damage to his back legs, when he fell off our bed. Now he has to sleep and snore in his own bed on the floor. Thankfully, with time and tender loving care, he is slowly healing.

Yoda brings so much pleasure to our lives. He is sweet natured, funny, and a wonderful companion. Brian is retired, so he and Yoda spend the whole day together while I am at work. They go for short walks, roam around the yard, take naps and watch Dog TV! When I get home, he greets me at the door bobbing his head, prancing, and snorting. He follows me around all over the place for thirty minutes, even if I pet him and talk to him a million times!

When I talk to him, he looks at me with those big brown eyes as if he knows what I am saying and he just doesn't know what to say back. He is such a pleasure to talk to. I think if he could talk he would have stories to tell. He indulges my need to be mothering and even lets me dress him up in funny hats for the holidays. He cracks us up when he eats with his snorting and carrying on as he enjoys his food. Sometimes he sneezes so hard he scares himself and jumps sideways. We can't help but laugh.

. . .

Our boy seems to have a caretaker's heart, too. When I got sick with a severe kidney infection, he was there for me the whole time as if he were taking care of me. I thought this was very sweet! The only way my back felt much better was to lie down on the floor. I put my head on Yoda's bed and he would lie there beside me. We would lie there together and sleep for hours. It was very comforting to be able to pet him and hold my hand on him. This went on for about a week, until I finally had to seek medical help.

The only time Yoda gets a little upset is when my fur grandbabies come over for babysitting. He doesn't like to share me. Fortunately, his teeth are very flat so he can't bite anyone, but that doesn't stop him from head butting them and getting slobber on their necks when he tries. He yaps at the girls to get back and leave him alone. He may be smaller, but they are very submissive to him and do as he says. When they are there we call him "Little Gestapo!"

Yoda also isn't very happy when he has to go outside in what he considers bad weather. He has a great time on nice days, and I love watching him having fun. He holds his head high, runs, and twists his body every which way. He loves to roll in the grass! It's a different story when the weather isn't nice. He hates going outdoors when it's rainy, snowy, too cold or too windy. Maybe it's because of what he went through when he was on his own in the winter. I got him little booties for when it snows, but he doesn't like those either. I took a video of him trying to walk in those boots. He kept turning around and looking at me as if to say, "Why are you doing this to me?"

. . .

All I can say is that my husband and I love this little guy to pieces! He is the best little fur baby in the world. We always pet him and tell him what a good boy he is and how much we love him. He soaks it up and gives us love in return. He loves to be close to his people and licks our noses and cheeks. When I look into his big, soulful, brown eyes all I see is love shining from them. I think we were meant to be together. The timing of my daughter-in-law sending me the pictures and my decision to walk into that shelter were not a coincidence, but an inspiration.

To me, a house is not a home without dog. Yoda is

such a blessing and a treasure. He needed a home and I needed a pet to love. Even if I don't have him for very long, I know he is not out there in the elements like he was, and we are giving him the very best home he could have for his last few years. Lord knows when he passes there will never be another him, but I would definitely get another senior dog.

Story by Leah Faith Blanford as told to Val Silver

A dog is the only thing on earth that loves you more than he loves himself.

~Author Unknown

Photo of Faith Blanford and Yoda

Dogs are minor angels, and I don't mean that facetiously. They love unconditionally, forgive immediately, are the truest of friends, willing to do anything that makes us happy, etcetera. If we attributed some of those qualities to a person we would say they are special. If they had ALL of them, we would call them angelic. But because it's "only" a dog, we dismiss them as sweet or funny but little more. However when you think about it, what are the things that we most like in another human being? Many times those qualities are seen in our dogs every single day–we're just so used to them that we pay no attention.

~Jonathan Carroll

FROM TRASH TO TREASURE

I'd like to tell you about a sweet little soul—one of God's furry children. However, in order to tell this story, I must bring you on a journey with me to see how God has worked in my life, and that of my animals, to venture our way to Suzie Q's rescue and ultimate freedom. I have many, what I call 'GOD' stories, but in this writing, I will stick to those involving animals.

God's marvelous plan for me began to unfurl many years ago, starting with Scooter, a sweet long haired Chihuahua, and a spunky, very talkative cat, my sweetheart, Bones. As happens, Scooter crossed the Rainbow Bridge and I was totally devastated; after 18 years together, I didn't think I would ever get over it. I was worried about Bones, too, who was just a year younger.

My nine year old granddaughter saw how sad I was, so when her father's fluffy Chihuahua had puppies, Jessie decided all by herself that I needed a new pup to help me get over my pain and sadness. Thus, our wonderful

Sweetie Pie arrived. This made me refocus from sadness to the trial of raising a new puppy at my already travelling age of 60 years. This was no easy task, but we got through it, and Sweetie Pie turned out to be a wonderful gift from God. A year later, and shortly after losing Bones, Sweetie Pie's sister, Angel, arrived as a tiny puppy on Christmas day.

God is connecting the dots—can you see? Sweetie Pie raised Angel and was a great role model. The two became totally bonded and they did everything together. I had never before had the wonderful opportunity to watch one pup totally train another.

Several years later, while working long distance for a rescue in New Jersey, we took in a peppy young Silky Terrier from the Camden County Animal Shelter. He had been hit by a vehicle and left to die on the street. We flew him into Georgia and named him Mr. Wiggles. He was a bit more than I could handle, but as we do with all of the rescues we adopt, we kept him anyway.

Next, while volunteering for a local Georgia rescue, I was asked by the director to foster a Chihuahua she had pulled the day he was to die. He was emaciated, beaten, scared and totally unadoptable. He hated men and was scared of everything. He needed a kind heart, a quiet atmosphere and a loving place to lay his head. Since we seem to be guided by God to collect the unwanted and discarded, we adopted him. Chalupa is our 'special' boy—he just 'is'. We don't ask much from him. He can be very hard to handle, and is extremely fearful to this day. He is incontinent, growls a lot and we think he probably has some brain damage. Regardless, we accept him for who he is and love him, and he knows that.

. . .

Now here is where my 'God' story gets interesting! At a young nine years of age, our much beloved Sweetie Pie got cancer and, of course, I was devastated. We also moved from Atlanta to Cumming, Georgia to a totally different environment and lifestyle. Luckily, God gave Sweetie Pie enough time to come to this house and enjoy just a bit a heaven on earth. She was progressing in her illness and her life was getting more taxing every day. It was a long haul of hospice and quite expensive for treatments that drained our bank account and didn't work. But as we all know, rescuers have big hearts and empty wallets; we would do anything for our Sweetie Pie.

Shortly after we moved to Cumming, we were on our way to an appointment when we saw a well groomed, healthy looking Bichon Frisé sitting on the side of our road. In the country, people are of a different mindset (something I still can't get used to); they allow their dogs and cats to run loose, so we were not sure if this was a neighbor pet or not. We decided that if he was still sitting there when we returned, we would take him. Sure enough, he was. We believe he had been dropped off on the side of that road and was waiting for his owner's return, as we know dogs do. Like most abandoned pups, he was very skittish. It took us three days to get him in the car. I would stand in the middle of the road stopping traffic while my husband tried to entice him with treats. Ahhh–finally he was safe!

We named the fluffy white dog Mr. Bean. He stayed with us for about three weeks. Having him in my life at that time took my focus off of what I know would have put me into a terrible, depressive state. This was God at work–taking care of me. I truly believe that God put Mr. Bean on that road so we could help each other. Two days after Sweetie Pie passed, we found him a wonderful, loving home. I still dog sit for him when his family travels.

The day after Mr. Bean left, my granddaughter Jessie called to tell me about a little Chihuahua camping on her porch, and asked what she should do. Again, I saw this as God at work keeping me busy. I picked up this poor, emaciated, sick little boy, named him Easton, and put him through heartworm treatment and some training before finding him a good home.

Penny came along six months later as a domestic abuse case. She was posted as a chi, but when I went to pick her up at the shelter, out walked an overweight terrier-sort, with long dirty fur that was falling out all over the place. Of course, I couldn't say no. I took her in, cleaned her up, had her shaved, and put her on a diet. She's bigger than I'm used to, but she fits right in and they all do well together.

. . .

Now, I was done—*or so I thought!* My family was complete

with Angel, Penny, Chalupa and Mr. Wiggles (from left to right) and I would just network animals on the internet for rescue. That is, until August, 2013, when this little dog, deemed a terrier, popped up on my screen. She was not a pretty girl–she had bulgy eyes, short hair, and I knew she probably was not a terrier. She wore a clunky collar that was way too big for her. I worked very hard trying to find a rescue or adopter for her. The facility was overflowing and her time was getting down to the wire. Amazingly enough, on this particular Wednesday, my husband had stayed home from work to take me to a doctor appointment. Knowing I really wanted to save this odd looking terrier, I asked him to come into my office and look at my computer. I showed him her picture, and wonder of wonders, he said, "Sure!"

This shelter just happens to be in the vicinity of my doctor, so we packed all of our dogs in the car and headed out. Jim sat in the car with the air conditioner running the whole time I was at my therapy, which is a good amount of time. We then left and went straight to the shelter. Out came this little, itty bitty, sad looking girl. She was quiet, coughing, and doing that backward sneezing really hard. They put my dogs in one bonding kennel and her in another. They seemed to tolerate each other. I was not going to let this little dog die, so of course we adopted her.

Because Suzie still needed to have her spaying and vaccinations, she had to wait until Friday to come home. I went back to the shelter at 11AM, and her veterinary appointment was at 4PM, making for a long, taxing day. We had lunch at Chic Fil-A, and she didn't even know what chicken was. She didn't like the crate, so eventually I took her out and she was quiet in the car. I noticed that she was extremely submissive and didn't relate at all. God bless our little Suzie Q–she had no personality! I took her to a pet store and bought her a tiny collar, a name tag, a leash, a harness and a bed, all in pink. Then we spent about an hour sitting in the back seat of my car while I used a whole container of wipes trying to get the stench off her. Someone's trash was becoming our treasure.

Our vet completely checked her over. She determined that Suzie Q was nine years old and had been a breeding dog her entire adult life–how many liters of puppies, she could not say. Suzie's lack of personality and total willingness to allow you to do anything you want to her was a good indication that she was made to be submissive and used as a machine. She also had a small tumor on one of her breasts that had a high chance of becoming cancerous if not removed. Unspayed females are at higher risk of illness and cancer, and have fewer puppies as they age. We suspect that because of her age and the fact that she was found wandering the streets with only one puppy, Suzie Q was no longer useful. She and her puppy were thrown away. This I see over and over again as a networker.

. . .

Saving Suzie Q turned out to be a very emotional journey for me. God used her rescue to take me down to some deep feelings that were unresolved in my life–sadness. Since she was a breeder girl, I realized that she had a much *boxed* life. She had no personality of her own; she was an empty shell. She didn't know about treats, regular food, a car ride, a yard or freedom of any kind. She crawled under beds, furniture or anything she could hide under; when you called her, she curled up and tried to hide. She did not bark.

Suzie's lack of personality and fear took me to a place I had never gone before, and I cried for her and myself (as I found out) for three days. I realized that this time around, God had me rescue myself. You see, I was abused for 20 years in my first marriage, and like Suzie Q, I had been a virtual prisoner.

My freedom came 20 years ago, and I had worked through a great deal of my feelings. However, when God put this tiny bug eyed, scrawny senior on my computer screen, and I decided to step up and be her angel, little did I know how she would affect me. Suzie Q's rescue was to take me down to a deep unresolved feeling of sadness that had remained unresolved and untouched from my past. Through Suzie, I was able to finally feel the sadness I suffered all those years.

As Suzie's hair began to grow, I could finally figure out what kind of dog she is–a full bred Shi Tzu. Her hair was shaved so short when she came in, that no one could tell. We think she may have been kept this way in order to keep and breed her without the mess of hair in the way. How sad.

· · ·

One of the important messages I want to share from this story of Suzie Q and all rescues is the value of adopting a shelter animal. When you take an animal from a shelter, you save two lives, the one you adopt and the one you just made room for.

You never know what you will learn from saving a shelter or rescue animal. For me, each rescue has taught me a different skill or lesson. I thought I was saving a life and giving them my heart, but I found out that my furry God children also give to me, be it by a lesson, skill or the opportunity to resolve unfinished feelings.

Thank you, God, for Suzie Q. As I say–we took someone else's trash and made her our TREASURE!

Story by Patti Mansfield

Animals are more than ever a test of our character, of mankind's capacity for empathy and for decent, honorable conduct and faithful stewardship. We are called to treat them with kindness, not because they have rights or power or some claim to equality, but in a sense because they don't; because they all stand unequal and powerless before us.

From *Dominion: The Power of Man, the Suffering of Animals, and the Call to Mercy* by Matthew Scully

Photo of Patti Mansfield and Suzie Q

It's hard not to immediately fall in love with a dog who has a good sense of humor.

~Kate DiCamillo, *Because of Winn-Dixie*

LIFE IS GOO(SE)D

A Story in Three Parts

I...
have a king-sized, soft-side, pillow-top, waveless waterbed, the kind with a twin bladder on each side.
I...
love this bed.

It's the kind of bed that just snugs you all up when you fall into it. The water beneath me keeps me cool while the goose down on top of me keeps me warm. Aaaah, it's a gooder.

I also have a ginormous black lab named Aiko.
I...
love this dog.

I rescued her from the Dumb Friends League when I was in Denver for a few days, taking a class for my job in Grand Junction. My kids and I had been looking, casually, in Junction for a dog, and had not found 'the one'. My first night at the hotel, I jumped on the internet to check out the shelters, and the dogs they had for adoption. I decided that after my training the following day, I would go to the shelter that had the most dogs I was interested in. After visiting with four or five dogs, I checked the notes and pictures I had printed, and asked about the last one, a Black Labrador Retriever called Amy.

"Oh, she's in quarantine," I'm told. "She has kennel cough."

I said "Well, let's go see her." It was love at first sight, as this dog lumbered towards me in a way that made me think for a second that I was mistakenly put in a room with a bear. Of all things, I learned that she had been transferred to DFL from the county I lived in, and they were really trying to find her a home. The tech literally jumped up and down for joy when I told her Amy was the one for me. I named her Aiko, which means "to love or to be loved".

Aiko...

loves *our* bed too.

A week ago this morning, I woke to a soaked floor and a deflated bladder. Not MY bladder, as it is always inflated upon waking. No, the bladder beneath me had sprung a leak.

Having just gone through this ordeal five months ago when Aiko caused a small hole on HER side of the bed, in HER bladder, I knew it was going to be a long week of draining, sopping up, drying, patching, hoisting, refilling, and sleeping on the couch. But that's ok, this bed is worth it.

The night before last, repair and reassembly was finally completed. I don't know who was more excited–me or Aiko. As my son and I were busy hoisting those heavy-as-sh** bladders back into the bed and refilling them, Aiko would come in and check on our progress, each time looking at me with those sad big brown puppy-dog eyes. I would say, "Not yet, Aiko," and she'd turn and slink back into the living room and lay on her blanket, which had been HER 'couch' all week. I wasn't the only one who had been displaced, and I wasn't the only one anxious to get back in that bed. Well, we got done; I made the bed, put one of Aiko's clean blankets on top of my comforter, and went in the living room.

She immediately lifted her head with her ears squared up, on alert, made and held eye contact with me (rare for her), waiting for the word. I said "It's ready, Aiko." She jumped up with lightning speed, which for her means she set into motion her 15-second 'get-myself-up-off-the-floor' process, and looked at me with a "you're not kiddin' me right now, right?" look on her face. She wagged her tail as she walked her 90-year-old-man pace to my room. She got to the foot of the bed, looked at me again as if to say, "Pinch me!" and started her climb up. She circled a couple of times and plopped down with a big, happy sigh.

It was a happy, peaceful night.

I left for work yesterday morning, chatted with my friend, mentioned my bed was back in business and how happy my dog was about that. She said, "You KNOW she's gonna spend her WHOLE day on that bed." Well, that's fine, gives me warm fuzzies knowing she's happy and comfortable and realizing that floor was pretty dang hard all week, extra-hard on her old bones, and doesn't she just totally deserve to spend the day in the bed.

Sooooo...

I had something to do last night after work, and got home around 9:00. I pulled into the garage thinking, "Aiko's gonna be mad her dinner's so late." I make my way to the door, thinking, "She's gonna be sitting right here on the other side of this door with that look on her face." (You know the look.)

I open the door and she's not sitting there, waiting for me. There are no lights on, and it is dark. I walk across the kitchen to hit the light, and she's STILL not there, weird, because I'm home! And...I'm in the KITCHEN where the food is, which is where SHE usually is, when that's where I am.

The light illuminates and I turn towards the living room, and there she is, lying on her blanket. But, something's...kind of weird, kind of...off. I make the corner and get closer and see all these little tufts of white, tufts on the floor, tufts all over. Aiko, she's lying there, not looking up, faking being asleep like we used to do when our parents would check on us after bedtime, and we're supposed to be asleep–you know how you'd fake it. I think, "Oh my gosh, she's killed a bird." I look around and see mounds of feathers. They are all over the place. "Oh my gosh, she's killed a FLOCK!" I realize at this point I'm really afraid to keep looking. I hate seeing dead things.

I go towards the back door to hit the light for the back yard, expecting to see a massacre. I imagine carnage, legs and beaks scattered everywhere. I imagine little cousin birds and neighbor birds perched on the fence, looking over the scene, weeping and tweeting "How could this happen?" to each other.

But there is nothing.

Then I go, "Uh, oh."

I look back at Aiko to catch her watching me. She shut her eyes real fast–back to that fake sleeping gig.

I walk into my room, following this trail of tufts of white that gets bigger and bigger as I approach my bed. I'm about halfway there, still expecting to find a big dead bird on my bed, and I'm holding my breath as I force myself to look.

Then I see, and I stand there, confused for a second, a little irritated for a flash, and then relieved there's no carcass. There's just a BIG pile of feathers, I mean BIG, and what used to be a pretty nice goose down comforter with the middle all ripped out of it. Yep, Aiko went goose hunting, with my comforter. She must have had a TIME, I'm telling ya'–feathers were still floating in the air, slowly making their ways down to settle back on the bed, the floor, the dresser, and me.

I giggle and just shake my head as I imagine the scene– Aiko with that comforter between her teeth, shaking her head and growling and ripping and clawing and snorting and bouncing in sheer delight, feathers flying and filling the air in my room. I turn to see Aiko sitting there in my doorway, ears squared up, on alert, feathers on her snout, soft wispy pieces of down hanging from her jowls, and in her little eyebrows, which shift hilariously up-and-down as she focuses her gaze on me from one eye to the other...it just added to it, and I just busted right up laughing!

Aiko and Me

Aiko was an overweight dog, older than her years. The vet thinks she was around six when we got her, three years before she went goose hunting on the bed in December of 2009. She was half deaf, incontinent the whole time we had her, had arthritis that worsened with age, suffered chronic ear infections, and for reasons unknown to me, she had a strong dislike for other dogs. Cats though, she'd sit and watch for hours. She loved riding in the car, head out the window and gums flapping in the wind. She also enjoyed walks, but not every day because sometimes she had trouble moving.

Aiko rescued me when I adopted her almost a year after I completed chemotherapy and radiation for breast cancer. She filled a void I did not know existed. It didn't take long with her in my life to feel my post-treatment depression lift, and she quickly became my drug of choice for treating it. I remember wishing several times that I had had Aiko during my trials and tribulations with cancer, as I know she would have made it less lonely and more tolerable.

She got that chance when my cancer recurred to my brain six years later. She had gotten older, I had gotten sicker, and we just chilled together. After just a few short months, though, Aiko got very sick. My kids and I lived in denial for a week or so; then we were forced to rescue my rescuer once more by relieving her of her struggle. She always loved going to the vet to watch the cats, but this time she was too sick to care. This was the first time she ever tried to keep from going into a room. It was as if somehow she knew. And she knew we knew. She seemed to know we were sharing HER world, but at the end, as bad as she felt, she did not want to leave OURS. It broke my heart. I was in such grief after losing her I almost thought I wouldn't make it. We cried buckets then, we still cry now, and we miss her dearly every day.

Life According to Aiko

Part of the fun of living with Aiko was learning her rules, which she made sure I knew. Her goose hunt is just one example of what might happen if those rules weren't followed. Here are a few more:

(Spoken nicely:) "I'll come to you if I want any loving. Otherwise, I'm fine where I'm at, and you're fine where you're at. But when I come to you, we WILL hold hands."

"I don't know why, but I don't like making eye contact very often. And I cannot, will not, eat or drink if you are in the same room; I will lie down in front of my food/water dish and wait for you to leave the room. I appreciate your cooperation."

"I hate, hate, hate other dogs. Keep them away from me, or else."

"I don't like to be left home alone. It's okay when you are at work, but in the evenings and on the weekends, by gosh, you better include me. Otherwise, expect me to get in the trash."

"If you leave the 20 pound Christmas ham on the counter to cool, I WILL stealthily get it down and sneak past you out through my doggie door with it." (This was a dog who could not jump on to the bed, could not jump into the car or out of it, could not stand on hind legs with front legs on someone. How she got stuff off the counter I will never know. If she got in the trash, she would take stuff out back and bury it. I'm still finding her treasures.)

Yes, life with Aiko was goo(se)d, and we wouldn't have had it any other way.

Story by Lee Lee Schmalz

EPILOGUE

When Lee Lee's daughter Erin moved out of the home she had shared with her dad and brother, she brought her eight year old schnauzer Cody to Lee Lee's house to live, because her new home did not have a fenced yard. Lee Lee wanted no part of having another dog–that is, until she met and fell in love with Cody, which took all of 20 minutes. She credits this loving, funny guy with helping her heal from Aiko's loss and her bout with brain cancer. No one expected her to beat the beast again, and her oncologists claim her case was "exceptional" and "amazing". She hopes to train Cody, who is now her dog, as a therapy dog. He appears to be a natural.

Dogs are our link to paradise. They don't know evil or jealousy or discontent. To sit with a dog on a hillside on a glorious afternoon is to be back in Eden, where doing nothing was not boring—it was peace.

~Milan Kundera

HOW YOU CAN HELP

Shelters and rescue organizations are in desperate need of many things. Funds and foster homes are usually in high demand. In addition, local shelters often welcome donations of food, hard rubber toys, treats, blankets, dog beds and more. Some organizations welcome volunteers. The best first step is to contact your local shelter and ask what they need. Often, you can find this information on their website.

Another way to help, right from the comfort of your home, is to like pages of rescue organizations and share their posts with your friends. When you see posts asking you to sign petitions against animal cruelty, sign them.

Most importantly, be a responsible pet guardian. Be part of the solution, not part of the problem. Spay and neuter your pets. It is estimated that for every human being, 13 dogs and 45 cats are born. Instead of breeding or buying puppy mill pups from pet stores, save a life and adopt from shelters and rescue organizations. Encourage others to do the same.

If you choose to have pets, adopt animals that are right for you and your family, and take care of them as cherished, life-long members of your family. If you can't commit for the long haul, but still want a dog or cat in your life, consider fostering, adopting an older senior, or going to the local shelter a few times a week to help out and give the animals there some much needed love and attention.

The Animals' Savior

I looked at all the caged animals in the shelter…
the cast-offs of human society.
I saw in their eyes love and hope, fear and dread,
sadness, and betrayal.
And I was angry.
"God," I said. "This is terrible!
Why don't you do something?"
God was silent for a moment, and then He
spoke softly,
"I have done something," He replied,
"I created you."

~Copyright 2001, Jim Willis, from *Pieces of My Heart: Writings Inspired by Animals and Nature*, www.crean.com/jimwillis.
Used with permission.

GIVING BACK

In appreciation for the unconditional love our animal friends give us, it is only fitting to give back to them and those working so hard to help them, in their time of need. As our way of giving back, several non-profit shelters and rescues will receive donations from the proceeds of this book for projects that will make life better for their residents, special needs, spaying and neutering, and expenses.

The nonprofit organizations receiving funds provide a safe, caring place of shelter for homeless dogs, actively pursue loving homes for eligible dogs, provide medical care, raise awareness about the needs of rescue pets, promote spaying, neutering and responsible pet ownership, raise awareness about puppy mills, need a financial helping hand to continue their mission successfully, and seek to make conditions as good as possible for the animals in their care. They were nominated by our writers and have agreed to be listed on our webpage.

Shelter, rescue, or animal welfare organizations interested in raising funds with *Rescue Me*, can contact us at http://tapinfinity.com/connect or through our Facebook page at www.facebook.com/rescuemetales.

. . .

If you like this book and support its mission, please post a review on Amazon and other book sites and tell others about it. Your support makes it possible for us to help homeless dogs and continue donating much needed funds. Thank you.

You can give without loving, but you cannot love without giving.

~Amy Carmichael

TEAM RESCUE CONTRIBUTORS

Val Silver lives in northern New York with her husband Scott and their dog Teddy. She lives a busy and fulfilling life as a grandmother, a Reading Recovery teacher, an energy healer, a holistic wellness coach and educator, and an advocate of animal welfare and dog rescue. Val regularly writes articles for her Holistic MindBody Healing website, blog, and for Bellesprit magazine. She is her happiest, best self when she feels connected with nature and dogs are part of her life.

Judith Ambrosio lives in New Jersey with her dog Frances. When she is not busy at her job as a commercial insurance/risk management and reinsurance professional, you will probably find her caring for friends and family in need, amusing Frances, or cruising on her Spyder motorcycle.

Julia Buie is an avid shelter and rescue dog activist and volunteer. Julia lives in Zuni, a small township within Isle of Wight County, VA. Recently, she and her husband welcomed a new addition to their family, a chubby pug named Pugsly (affectionately referred to as Pugalicious). Julia invites you to friend her on Facebook and to become part of her mission. She encourages you to share the photos and stories of dogs in need like she does. Who knows? Maybe you too will find your new passion in life.

Karal Gregory is a freelance writer and photographer at The Orange Chair and Karal Gregory Photography. Karal was rescued in 2002 by a sweet little beagle named Pearl. She became involved in animal rescue and activism after moving to LA and volunteering with Tails of the City Animal Rescue. She is a corporate sponsor and supporter of the Beagle Freedom Project and works with Virginia-based Bay Beagle Rescue and Beagles to the Rescue. She currently resides in Ojai, California, sharing her space with her three misfit hounds, Daisy, Isabel, and Tyler, and one hound figurine keeping watch from the nightstand.

Sandra Smith lives in northern New York with her husband Walter and their dogs Leonardo, Peanut and Julie. Sandra is a Reiki master and a licensed aesthetician with advanced certification in oncology aesthetics. She writes a monthly skin care column for Bellesprit magazine. Sandi devotes her life to sharing the gift of healing with others and caring for her furry and human loved ones.

Kim Massey lives in Louisville, Kentucky. She is an active member of the Heart to Heart Rescue network; a nationwide non-profit organization dedicated to rescuing homeless and abandoned animals, primarily dogs from high-kill shelters and from owners who can no longer care for them.

Letha Hundley lives in Virginia with her dogs Winnie and Sammy, and three FIV+ cats. She is an avid animal lover and an advocate for senior pet adoption. Letha credits her dogs for healing her heart and putting a smile back on her face.

Leah Faith Blanford is an ordained non-denominational Christian minister in the state of Virginia. She and her husband Brian have been married for 35 years. She is the proud mother of two grown children, Shawn & Rhiannon, who have blessed her with four wonderful grandchildren. My Lord, family and my sweet Yoda are the center of my life. Faith has been happily employed with the Evelyn Ott School of Dance as secretary / receptionist for the past 22 years. The most fulfilling aspect of this job is watching children learn and grow with the art form and meeting great families along the way.

Patti Mansfield is retired from her own company and now dedicates most of her time to animal advocacy and rescue. Patti lives in Cumming, Georgia and has five rescue dogs of her own; bringing in a stray here and there to get them ready to find their forever homes. She is joined by her husband Jim, who totally supports her rescue efforts. Patti has three children, five grandchildren and three great grandchildren. One of her daughters is high profile rescuer with Lilo's Promise Animal Rescue in New Jersey.

Lee Lee Schmalz works in human resources at Colorado Mesa University and volunteers at her local hospital as a cancer patient advocate. She lives in Grand Junction, Colorado with a daughter who returned to the empty nest, along with her schnauzer, Cody.

RESOURCES

The Rescue Me Webpage hosts the audios and videos featured in this book, photos, our shelter or rescue of the month, an up-to-date list of sponsored organizations, and a link to related articles. (tapinfinity.com/rescue-me/)

Be a Hero for Animals by Val Silver is your free pdf companion guide including 15+ ways to make a positive impact for homeless dogs and other animals from the comforts of home. Discover how to be a voice for the voiceless, make donations of food and care for free, and more. Get yours here: tapinfinity.com/hero

The Animal Rescue site is the place to take free actions that make a big difference for animals in rescues and shelters. Click on the purple link at the top of the page every day to provide free food for homeless animals, vote for your favorite shelters to win cash, sign petitions and more. (theanimalrescuesite.greatergood.com)

Petfinder.com has a database of over 372,000 adoptable shelter and rescue pets from over 13,606 adoption groups in the United States and Canada. Petfinder is also an excellent source of information about how to choose and care for your pets, where to find organizations near you, and how to help other pets in need. (www.petfinder.com)

Adoptapet.com helps you find dogs and cats available for adoption nationwide. Learn how to care for your new friend, find rescue groups near you, and lend a helping hand. (www.adoptapet.com)

Petango.com offers a real time search service of adoptable pets in thousands of animal welfare locations across North America. Their blog features posts on animal health, behavior, and safety. (www.petango.com)

ASPCA.org provides extensive information about fighting animal cruelty, how you can get involved, caring for your pets, training, and correcting minor and serious behavior problems. Before giving up your pet because of behavioral concerns, put their advice into action. For serious concerns, call their behavior hotline at (212) 876-7700, extension 4357. (www.aspca.org)

No Kill Nation is a non-profit organization with a shared purpose of working toward the goal of eliminating the mass killing of homeless animals. Find them on Facebook. (https://www.facebook.com/nokillcoalition)

Facebook is a great place to hook up with people in rescue. Just search by type of animal plus rescue (i.e.: dogs+ rescue, dachshunds+rescue). When you find a page you like, click the like button to follow and share their posts. Facebook has made it possible to rescue as many as an additional million animals per year. There are hundreds of shelters which do not allow public access, and with the use of Facebook, rescuers are now able to post pictures of these animals and find rescues and homes for them. They also alert the public to scammers and abusers, lost animals, food recalls and more. Read more at http://tapinfinity.com/advocating/

Like us on Facebook at
www.facebook.com/rescuemetales

What's Your Story?

Use these pages to record your favorite memories and lessons learned from your animal friends.